Security Strategy and Regional Security Arrangements

Security Strategy and Regional Security Arrangements

H.G. Joshi

FORWARD BOOKS
New Delhi • Guwahati • Visakhapatnam

FORWARD BOOKS
4649-B/21, Ansari Road
Darya Ganj, New Delhi - 110 002
Ph.: 23263193 / 9811582579 / 09435116718
Fax: 011-23263193
Email: ektabooks@yahoo.com
www.akanshapublishinghouse.com

Security Strategy and Regional Security Arrangements

First Published 2011
ISBN 978-81-909742-7-1

PRINTED IN INDIA

Published by Forward Books, New Delhi and Printed at Harmain Offset Press, Delhi.

To
Those Brave Soldiers
working in UN Peacekeeping forces
in different parts of the world,
this book is humbly dedicated.

Contents

Preface

> "A man of a right spirit is not a man of narrow and private views but is greatly interested and concerned for the good of the community to which he belongs, and particularly of the city or village in which he resides, and for the true welfare of the society of which he is member."
>
> —*Jonathan Edwards*

The notion of national security is important in the political arena as every nation-state deeply intends to protect its autonomy and sovereignty as well as national identity. Most often security of one nation is threatened by other state(s) on one pretext or other. Causes may be real or virtual. Every nation-state has its security and defence mechanism. But keeping in view the mutual interest collective efforts by like-minded or vested interests are being made on regional basis. Thus emerged many security arrangements and regional alliances in different parts of the globe. It is pertinent to note that in regional security arrangements, with changing circumstances every time new equations are established which may lose meaning with passage of time thus become part of oblivion.

Security strategy and regional security arrangements are widely debated and researched topics by scholars of repute in the field of defence studies, political science and international relations. A plethora of literature is already there and more is pouring in regularly. This endeavour is unique which compiles vital readings on the topic. The judiciously selected writings are gathered under the following chapters—Introduction; Global Security: Concepts and Prospects; National Security: Concept and Issues; International Peace and Security; Regional Security Arrangements; Subregional Agenda for Peace in Central Africa; Latin America and the Caribbean: Strategic Cooperation; Disarmament: Significance and Relevance; Military and Strategic Security and Bibliography etc.

Hopefully, students, scholars and policy planners will find this of utility.

In course of preparing this work, I have consulted a number of books, articles, monographs and reports, penned by eminent scholars in the field. Websites are other digital sources also proved helpful. Admittedly, the credit for this ought go to them in true sense of spirit. I owe a great debt to them all. My friends and colleagues have always been instrumental in my such creativity. I express my gratitude to them also. Last but not least I am thankful to my publishers for evincing interest in this work and materialising it in such an elegant manner.

Constructive criticism and suggestion are welcome from all learned readers to make it more comprehensive and informative.

—HGJ

1

Introduction

> "Despair is the absolute extreme of self-love. It is reached when a man deliberately turns his back on all help from anyone else in order to taste the rotten luxury of knowing himself to be lost."
>
> —*Thomas Merton*

'Security', 'national security' and 'regional security arrangements' are much debated topics these days. Since in the present book we have taken the theme of national security and regional security system, first it is important to have the full understanding of security.

We will discuss security in different realms. But our main focus will be security in reference to defence and national security.

Etymologically, by the term security we mean the degree of protection against danger, damage, loss, and criminal activity. Security as a form of protection are *structures and processes that provide or improve security as a condition.* The Institute for Security and Open Methodologies (ISECOM) in the OSSTMM defines security as "a form of protection where a separation is created between the assets and the threat". This includes but is not limited to the elimination of either the asset or the threat.

Security as a national condition was defined in a United Nations study (1986), so that countries can develop and progress safely. Security has to be compared to related concepts: safety, continuity, reliability. The key difference between security and reliability is that security must take into account the actions of people attempting to cause destruction.

Why Security

- **With respect to classified matter, the condition that prevents unauthorized persons from having access to official information that is safeguarded in the interests of national security.**
- **Measures taken by a military unit, an activity or installation to protect itself against all acts designed to, or which may.**

Here it is pertinent to note that perception of security is sometimes poorly mapped to measureable objective security. The perceived effectiveness of security measures is sometimes different from the actual security provided by those measures. The presence of security protections may even be taken for security itself. For example, two computer security programs could be interfering with each other and even cancelling each other's effect, while the owner believes s/he is getting double the protection.

Similarly, security theater is a critical term for deployment of measures primarily aimed at raising subjective security in a population without a genuine or commensurate concern for the effects of that measure on—and possibly decreasing—objective security. For example, some consider the screening of airline passengers based on static databases to have been Security Theater and Computer Assisted Passenger Prescreening System to have created a *decrease* in objective security. Perception of security can also increase objective security when it affects or deters malicious behavior, as with visual signs of security protections, such as video surveillance, alarm systems in a home, or an anti-theft system in a car such as a LoJack, signs.

Since some intruders will decide not to attempt to break into such areas or vehicles, there can actually be less damage to windows in addition to protection of valuable objects inside. Without such advertisement, a car-thief might, for example, approach a car, break the window, and then flee in response to an alarm being triggered. Either way, perhaps the car itself and the objects inside aren't stolen, but with *perceived security* even the windows of the car have a lower chance of being damaged, increasing the financial security of its owner(s).

However, the non-profit, security research group, ISECOM, has determined that such signs may actually increase the violence, daring, and desperation of an intruder This claim shows that perceived security works mostly on the provider and is not security at all. It is important, however, for signs advertising security not to give clues as to how to subvert that security, for example in the case where a home burglar might be more likely to break into a certain home if he or she is able to learn beforehand which company makes its security system.

It is significant to not ethat there is an immense literature on the analysis and categorisation of security. Part of the reason for this is that, in most security systems, the "weakest link in the chain" is the most important. The situation is asymmetric since the *defender* must cover all points of attack while the attacker need only identify a single weak point upon which to concentrate.

Types of Security

Information Technology

- Application security
- Computing security
- Data security
- Information security
- Network security

Physical Realm

- Airport security
- Port security/Supply chain security
- Food security
- Home security
- Hospital security
- Physical security
- School security
- Shopping centre security
- Infrastructure security

Political

- Homeland security
- Human security
- International security
- National security
- Public security

Monetary

- Financial security
- Aviation security is a combination of material and human resources and measures intended to counter unlawful interference with aviation.
- Operations Security (OPSEC) is a complement to other "traditional" security measures that evaluates the organization from an adversarial perspective.

Security Management in Organizations

In the corporate world, various aspects of security were historically addressed separately - notably by distinct and often noncommunicating departments for IT security, physical security, and fraud prevention. Today there is a greater recognition of the interconnected nature of security requirements, an approach variously known as holistic security, "all hazards" management, and other terms.

Inciting factors in the convergence of security disciplines include the development of digital video surveillance technologies (see Professional video over IP) and the digitization and networking of physical control systems (see SCADA). Greater interdisciplinary cooperation is further evidenced by the February 2005 creation of the Alliance for Enterprise Security Risk Management, a joint venture including leading associations in security (ASIS), information security (ISSA, the Information Systems Security Association), and IT audit (ISACA, the Information Systems Audit and Control Association).

Now we will put light on various elements and relevant aspects of security.

VULNERABILITY

In common parlance, by vulnerability we mean the susceptibility of a person, group, society or system to physical or emotional injury or attack. The term can also refer to a person who lets their guard down, leaving themselves open to censure or criticism. Vulnerability refers to a person's state of being liable to succumb to manipulation, persuasion, temptation etc.

Common Applications

In relation to hazards and disasters, vulnerability is a concept that links the relationship that people have with their environment to social forces and institutions and the cultural values that sustain and contest them.

"The concept of vulnerability expresses the multidimensionality of disasters by focusing attention on the totality of relationships in a given social situation which constitute a condition that, in combination with environmental forces, produces a disaster".

It's also the extent to which changes could harm a system, or to which a community can be affected by the impact of a hazard. In global warming, vulnerability is the degree to which a system is susceptible to, or unable to cope with, adverse effects of climate change, including climate variability and extremes.

It is pertinent to note that vulnerability research covers a complex, multidisciplinary field including development and poverty studies, public health, climate studies, security studies, engineering, geography, political ecology, and disaster and risk management. This research is of particular importance and interest for organizations trying to reduce vulnerability – especially as related to poverty and other Millennium Development Goals.

Many institutions are conducting interdisciplinary research on vulnerability. A forum that brings many of the current researchers on vulnerability together is the Expert Working Group (EWG). Researchers are currently working to refine definitions of "vulnerability", measurement and assessment methods, and effective communication of research to decision makers (Birkmann et al. 2006).

Within the body of literature related to vulnerability, major research streams include questions of methodology, such as: measuring and assessing vulnerability, including finding appropriate indicators for various aspects of vulnerability, up- and downscaling methods, and participatory methods (Villagran 2006).

Remarkably, a sub-category of vulnerability research is social vulnerability, where increasingly researchers are addressing some of the problems of complex human interactions, vulnerability of specific groups of people, and the impact of shocks from natural hazards, climate change, and other kinds of disruptions upon the human community. The importance of the issue is indicated by the establishment of endowed chairs at university departments to examine social vulnerability.

Military Vulnerability

In military terminology, vulnerability is a form of survivability, the others being susceptibility and recoverability. Vulnerability is defined in various ways depending on the nation and service arm concerned, but in general it refers to the near-instantaneous effects of a weapon attack. In some definitions, recoverability (damage control, firefighting, restoration of capability) is included in vulnerability.

Expert Working Group on Vulnerability

The Expert Working Group on Vulnerability is a group of experts brought together by the United Nations University Institute of Environment and Human Security (UNU-EHS). The overall goal of the Expert Working Group is to advance the concept of human security regarding vulnerability of societies to hazards of natural origin. The EWG exchanges ideas about the development of methodologies, approaches and indicators to measure vulnerability. This is a key task to build a bridge between the theoretical conceptualization of vulnerability and its practical application in decision-making processes.

The Expert Working Group is an exchange platform for experts and practitioners from various scientific backgrounds and world regions dealing with the identification and measurement of vulnerability. Emphasis is given to the identification of the different features and characteristics of vulnerability, coping capacities and adaptation strategies of different social groups, economic sectors and environmental components.

THREAT

A threat is an act of coercion wherein an act is proposed to elicit a negative response. It is a communicated intent to inflict harm or loss on another person. It is a crime in many jurisdictions.

In Brazil, the crime of threatening someone, defined as a threat to cause unjust and grave harm, is punishable by a fine or three months to one year in prison, as described in the Brazilian Penal Code, article 147. Brazilian jurisprudence does not treat as a crime a threat that was proferred in a heated discussion.

The German *Strafgesetzbuch* § 241 punishes the crime of threat with a prison term for up to one year or a fine.

In the United States, federal law criminalizes certain true threats transmitted via the U.S. mail or in interstate commerce. It also criminalizes threatening the government officials of the United States. Some U.S. states criminalize cyberbullying.

Libertarians hold that a palpable, immediate, and direct threat of aggression, embodied in the initiation of an overt act, is equivalent to aggression itself, and that proportionate defensive force would be justified in response to such a threat, if a clear and present danger exists.

RISK

Risk is the potential that a chosen action or activity (including the choice of inaction) will lead to a loss (an undesirable outcome). The notion implies that a choice having an influence on the outcome exists (or existed). Potential losses themselves may also be called "risks". Almost any human endeavour carries some risk, but some are much more risky then others.

For the sociologist Niklas Luhmann the term 'risk' is a neologism that appeared with the transition from traditional to modern society. "In the Middle Ages the term *risicum* was used in highly specific contexts, above all sea trade and its ensuing legal problems of loss and damage." In the vernacular languages of the 16th century the words *rischio* and *riezgo* were used. This was introduced to continental Europe, through interaction with Middle Eastern and North African Arab traders. In the English language the term *risk* appeared only in the 17th century, and "seems to be imported from continental Europe." When the terminology of *risk* took ground, it replaced the older notion that thought "in terms of good and bad fortune." Niklas Luhmann (1996) seeks to explain this transition: "Perhaps, this was simply a loss of plausibility of the old rhetorics of *Fortuna* as an allegorical figure of religious content and of *prudentia* as a (noble) virtue in the emerging commercial society."

Scenario analysis matured during Cold War confrontations between major powers, notably the United States and the Soviet Union. It became widespread in insurance circles in the 1970s when major oil tanker disasters forced a more comprehensive foresight. The scientific approach to risk entered finance in the 1960s with the advent of the capital asset pricing model and became increasingly important in the 1980s when financial derivatives proliferated. It reached general professions in the 1990s when the power of personal computing allowed for widespread data collection and numbers crunching.

Governments are using it, for example, to set standards for environmental regulation, e.g. "pathway analysis" as practiced by the United States Environmental Protection Agency.

Definitions of Risk

There are different definitions of risk for each of several applications. The widely inconsistent and ambiguous use of the word is one of several current criticisms of the methods to manage risk.

In one definition, "risks" are simply future issues that can be avoided or mitigated, rather than present problems that must be immediately addressed.

The simple fact is that risk is always a probability issue. Possibility is a binary condition – either something is possible, or it's not – 100% or 0%. Probability reflects the continuum between absolute certainty and impossibility. The key thing to keep in mind is that establishing probabilities is not the same thing as foretelling the future.

According to Factor Analysis of Information Risk, risk is:

> The probable frequency and probable magnitude of future loss.

In risk management, the term "hazard" is used to mean an event that could cause harm and the term "risk" is used to mean simply the probability of something happening.

OHSAS (Occupational Health & Safety Advisory Services) defines risk as the product of the probability of a hazard resulting in an adverse event, times the severity of the event.

There are many formal methods used to assess or to "measure" risk, which many consider to be a critical factor in human decision making. Some of these quantitative definitions of risk are well-grounded in sound statistics theory. However, these measurements of risk rely on failure occurrence data which may be sparse. This makes risk assessment difficult in hazardous industries such as nuclear energy where the frequency of failures is rare and harmful consequences of failure are astronomical. The dangerous harmful consequences often necessitate actions to reduce the probability of failure to infinitesimally small values which are hard to measure and corroborate with empirical evidence. Often, the probability of a negative event is estimated by using the frequency of past similar events or by event-tree methods, but probabilities for rare failures may be difficult to estimate if an event tree cannot be formulated. Methods to calculate the cost of the loss of human life vary depending on the purpose of the calculation. Specific methods include what people are willing to pay to insure against death, and radiological release (e.g., GBq of radio-iodine).

Financial risk is often defined as the unexpected variability or volatility of returns and thus includes both potential worse-than-expected as well as better-than-expected returns. References to negative risk below should be read as applying to positive impacts or opportunity (e.g., for "loss" read "loss or gain") unless the context precludes this interpretation.

In information security risk is defined as *the potential that a given threat will exploit vulnerabilities of an asset or group of assets and thereby cause harm to the organization*, an example being: Our desktop computers (asset) can be compromised by malware (threat) entering the environment as an email attachment (vulnerability).

The risk is then assessed as a function of three variables:

1. the probability that there is a threat
2. the probability that there are any vulnerabilities
3. the potential impact to the business.

The two probabilities are sometimes combined and are also known as likelihood. If any of these variables approaches zero, the overall risk approaches zero.

Risk Versus Uncertainty

Risk: Combination of the likelihood of an occurrence of a hazardous event or exposure(s) and the severity of injury or ill health that can be caused by the event or exposure(s)

In his seminal work *Risk, Uncertainty, and Profit*, Frank Knight (1921) established the distinction between risk and uncertainty.

> "... Uncertainty must be taken in a sense radically distinct from the familiar notion of Risk, from which it has never been properly separated. The term "risk," as loosely used in everyday speech and in economic discussion, really covers two things which, functionally at least, in their causal relations to the phenomena of economic organization, are categorically different. ... The essential fact is that "risk" means in some cases a quantity susceptible of measurement, while at other times it is something distinctly not of this character; and there are far-reaching and crucial differences in the bearings of the phenomenon depending on which of the two is really present and operating. ... It will appear that a measurable uncertainty, or "risk" proper, as we shall use the term, is so far different from an unmeasurable one that it is not in effect an uncertainty at all. We ... accordingly restrict the term "uncertainty" to cases of the non-quantitive type.:"

Thus, Knightian uncertainty is immeasurable, not possible to calculate, while in the Knightian sense risk is measurable.

Another distinction between risk and uncertainty is proposed in *How to Measure Anything: Finding the Value of Intangibles in Business* and *The Failure of Risk Management: Why It's Broken and How to Fix It* by Doug Hubbard:

Uncertainty: The lack of complete certainty, that is, the existence of more than one possibility. The "true" outcome/state/result/value is not known.

Measurement of uncertainty: A set of probabilities assigned to a set of possibilities. Example: "There is a 60% chance this market will double in five years"

Risk: A state of uncertainty where some of the possibilities involve a loss, catastrophe, or other undesirable outcome.

Measurement of risk: A set of possibilities each with quantified probabilities and quantified losses. Example: "There is a 40% chance the proposed oil well will be dry with a loss of $12 million in exploratory drilling costs".

In this sense, Hubbard uses the terms so that one may have uncertainty without risk but not risk without uncertainty. We can be uncertain about the winner of a contest, but unless we have some personal stake in it, we have no risk. If we bet money on the outcome of the contest, then we have a risk. In both cases there are more than one outcome. The measure of uncertainty refers only to the probabilities assigned to outcomes, while the measure of risk requires both probabilities for outcomes and losses quantified for outcomes.

Risk as a Vector Quantity

Hubbard also argues that defining risk as the product of impact and probability presumes (probably incorrectly) that the decision makers are risk neutral. Only for a risk neutral person is the "certain monetary equivalent" exactly equal to the probability of the loss times the amount of the loss. For example, a risk neutral person would consider 20% chance of winning $1 million exactly equal to $200,000 (or a 20% chance of losing $1 million to be exactly equal to losing $200,000). However, most decision makers are not actually risk neutral and would not consider these equivalent choices. This gave rise to Prospect theory and Cumulative prospect theory. Hubbard proposes instead that risk is a kind of "vector quantity" that does not collapse the probability and magnitude of a risk by presuming anything about the risk tolerance of the decision maker. Risks are simply described as a set or function of possible loss amounts each associated with specific probabilities. How this array is collapsed into a single value cannot be done until the risk tolerance of the decision maker is quantified.

Risk can be both negative and positive, but it tends to be the negative side that people focus on. This is because some things can be dangerous, such as putting their own or someone else's life at risk. Risks concern people as they think that they will have a negative effect on their future.

Information Technology Risk

Information technology risk, or IT risk, IT-related risk, is a risk related to information technology. This relatively new term due to an increasing awareness that information security is simply one facet of a multitude of risks that are relevant to IT and the real world processes it supports.

The increasing dependencies of modern society on information and computers networks (both in private and public sectors, including military) has led to a new terms like IT risk and Cyberwarfare.

Information Security Risk

Information security means protecting information and information systems from unauthorized access, use, disclosure, disruption, modification, perusal, inspection, recording or destruction.

Information security grew out of practices and procedures of computer security.

Information security has grown to Information assurance (IA) i.e. is the practice of managing risks related to the use, processing, storage, and transmission of information or data and the systems and processes used for those purposes.

While focused dominantly on information in digital form, the full range of IA encompasses not only digital but also analog or physical form.

Information assurance is interdisciplinary and draws from multiple fields, including accounting, fraud examination, forensic science, management science, systems engineering, security engineering, and criminology, in addition to computer science.

So, IT Risk is narrowly focused on Computer Security, while Information Security extends on risks related to other forms of information (paper, microfilm). Information Assurance risks include the ones related to the consistency of the business information stored in IT systems and the one stored on other means and the relevant business consequences.

Economic Risk

Economic risks can be manifested in lower incomes or

higher expenditures than expected. The causes can be many, for instance, the hike in the price for raw materials, the lapsing of deadlines for construction of a new operating facility, disruptions in a production process, emergence of a serious competitor on the market, the loss of key personnel, the change of a political regime, or natural disasters. Reference class forecasting was developed to eliminate or reduce economic risk.

The risks are evaluated using fault tree/event tree techniques. Where these risks are low, they are normally considered to be "Broadly Acceptable". A higher level of risk (typically up to 10 to 100 times what is considered Broadly Acceptable) has to be justified against the costs of reducing it further and the possible benefits that make it tolerable—these risks are described as "Tolerable if ALARP". Risks beyond this level are classified as "Intolerable".

The level of risk deemed Broadly Acceptable has been considered by regulatory bodies in various countries—an early attempt by UK government regulator and academic F. R. Farmer used the example of hill-walking and similar activities, which have definable risks that people appear to find acceptable. This resulted in the so-called Farmer Curve of acceptable probability of an event versus its consequence.

The technique as a whole is usually referred to as Probabilistic Risk Assessment (PRA) (or Probabilistic Safety Assessment, PSA). See WASH-1400 for an example of this approach.

In Public Works

In a peer reviewed study of risk in public works projects located in twenty nations on five continents, Flyvbjerg, Holm, and Buhl (2002, 2005) documented high risks for such ventures for both costs and demand. Actual costs of projects were typically higher than estimated costs; cost overruns of 50% were common, overruns above 100% not uncommon. Actual demand was often lower than estimated; demand shortfalls of 25% were common, of 50% not uncommon.

Due to such cost and demand risks, cost-benefit analyses of public works projects have proved to be highly uncertain.

The main causes of cost and demand risks were found to be optimism bias and strategic misrepresentation. Measures identified to mitigate this type of risk are better governance through incentive alignment and the use of reference class forecasting.

In Human Services

Huge ethical and political issues arise when human beings themselves are seen or treated as 'risks', or when the risk decision making of people who use human services might have an impact on that service. The experience of many people who rely on human services for support is that 'risk' is often used as a reason to prevent them from gaining further independence or fully accessing the community, and that these services are often unnecessarily risk averse.

Framing

Framing is a fundamental problem with all forms of risk assessment. In particular, because of bounded rationality (our brains get overloaded, so we take mental shortcuts), the risk of extreme events is discounted because the probability is too low to evaluate intuitively. As an example, one of the leading causes of death is road accidents caused by drunk driving—partly because any given driver frames the problem by largely or totally ignoring the risk of a serious or fatal accident.

For instance, an extremely disturbing event (an attack by hijacking, or moral hazards) may be ignored in analysis despite the fact it has occurred and has a nonzero probability. Or, an event that everyone agrees is inevitable may be ruled out of analysis due to greed or an unwillingness to admit that it is believed to be inevitable. These human tendencies for error and wishful thinking often affect even the most rigorous applications of the scientific method and are a major concern of the philosophy of science.

All decision-making under uncertainty must consider cognitive bias, cultural bias, and notational bias: No group of people assessing risk is immune to "groupthink": acceptance of obviously wrong answers simply because it is socially painful to disagree, where there are conflicts of interest. One effective way to solve framing problems in risk assessment or measurement (although some argue that risk cannot be measured, only assessed) is to raise others' fears or personal ideals by way of completeness.

Neurobiology of Framing

Framing involves other information that affects the outcome of a risky decision. The right prefrontal cortex has been shown to take a more global perspective while greater left prefrontal activity relates to local or focal processing

From the Theory of Leaky Modules McElroy and Seta proposed that they could predictably alter the framing effect by the selective manipulation of regional prefrontal activity with finger tapping or monaural listening. The result was as expected. Rightward tapping or listening had the effect of narrowing attention such that the frame was ignored. This is a practical way of manipulating regional cortical activation to affect risky decisions, especially because directed tapping or listening is easily done.

Fear as Intuitive Risk Assessment

For the time being, people rely on their fear and hesitation to keep them out of the most profoundly unknown circumstances.

In *The Gift of Fear*, Gavin de Becker argues that "True fear is a gift. It is a survival signal that sounds only in the presence of danger. Yet unwarranted fear has assumed a power over us that it holds over no other creature on Earth. It need not be this way."

Risk could be said to be the way we collectively measure and share this "true fear"—a fusion of rational doubt, irrational fear, and a set of unquantified biases from our own experience.

The field of behavioral finance focuses on human risk-aversion, asymmetric regret, and other ways that human financial behavior varies from what analysts call "rational". Risk in that case is the degree of uncertainty associated with a return on an asset.

Recognizing and respecting the irrational influences on human decision making may do much to reduce disasters caused by naive risk assessments that pretend to rationality but in fact merely fuse many shared biases together.

COUNTERMEASURE

Countermeasure is a measure or action taken to counter or offset another one. As a general concept it implies precision, and is any technological or tactical solution or system (often for a military application) designed to prevent an undesirable outcome in the process. The first known use of the term is in 1923.

Countermeasures can refer to the following disciplinary spectrum:

- defense
- medicine
- materials engineering
- electro-magnetic engineering
- policing
- Information technology
- Law
- Diplomatic security
- Pollution prevention

Defense countermeasures are often subdivided into "active" and "passive" countermeasures.

"Active" countermeasures that alter the electromagnetic, acoustic or other signature(s) of a target thereby altering the tracking and sensing behavior of an incoming threat (e.g., guided missile) are designated softkill measures. Measures that physically counterattack an incoming threat thereby destroying/altering its payload/warhead in such a way that the intended effect on the target is majorly impeded are designated hardkill measures. Both are further described in active protection systems.

"Passive" countermeasures include:

- Armor
- Camouflage
- Fortification
- Self-sealing fuel tank

DEFENCE IN DEPTH

It is pertinent to note that defence in depth is a military strategy; it seeks to delay rather than prevent the advance of an attacker, buying time and causing additional casualties by yielding space. Rather than defeating an attacker with a single, strong defensive line, defence in depth relies on the tendency of an attack to lose momentum over a period of time or as it covers a larger area. A defender can thus yield lightly defended territory in an effort to stress an attacker's logistics or spread out a numerically superior attacking force.

Once an attacker has lost momentum or is forced to spread out to pacify a large area, defensive counter-attacks can be mounted on the attacker's weak points with the goal being to cause attrition warfare or drive the attacker back to its original starting position. The idea of defence in depth is now widely used to describe non-military strategies as well.

Military Defence in Depth

It is apt to mention that a conventional defence strategy would concentrate all military resources at a front line which, if breached by an attacker, would leave the remaining defenders in danger of being outflanked and surrounded and would leave supply lines communications and command vulnerable. Defence in depth requires that a defender deploy his resources, such as fortifications, field works and military units at and well behind the front line.

Although an attacker may find it easier to breach the more weakly defended front line, as he advances he continues to meet resistance. As he penetrates deeper, the attacker's flanks become vulnerable, and, should the advance stall, the attacker risks being enveloped. The defence in depth strategy is particularly effective against an attacker who is able to concentrate his forces and attack a small number of places on an extended defensive line. Defenders who can fall back to a succession of prepared positions can extract a high price from the advancing enemy while themselves avoiding the danger of being overrun or outflanked.

Delaying the enemy advance mitigates the attacker's advantage of surprise and allows time to move defending units to make a defence and to prepare a counter-attack. A well-planned defence in depth strategy will deploy forces in mutually supportive positions and in appropriate roles. For example, poorly trained troops may be deployed in static defences at the front line, whereas better trained and equipped troops form a mobile reserve.

Successive layers of defence may use different technologies or tactics; for example, a row of dragon's teeth may be a problem for tanks but no barrier to infantry, while another barrier of wire entanglements has the opposite effects. Defence in depth may allow a defender to maximise the defensive possibilities of natural terrain and other advantages. The disadvantages of defence in depth are that it may be unacceptable for a defender to plan to give ground to an attacker.

This may be because vital military or economic resources are close to the front line or because yielding to an enemy is unacceptable for political or cultural reasons. Besides, the continuous retreats required by defence in depth require the defender to have a high degree of mobility in order to retreat successfully and the morale to recover from the retreat.

Remarkably, an early example of this came at the Battle of Cannae in 216 B.C. when Hannibal employed this maneuver in order to encircle and destroy 10 Roman Legions all at once, resulting in the largest single slaughter of Roman troops in the history of the republic. Later examples of defence in depth might be European hill forts and the development of concentric castles. In these examples, the inner layers of defence can support the outer layers with missile fire and an attacker must breach each line of defence in turn with the prospect of significant losses, whereas the defenders have the option of falling back to fight again.

In the American Revolutionary War Battle of Cowpens, the American forces were positioned in three lines which soaked up the shock of the British charge and inflicted heavy casualties before the Americans were able to overrun the British, who at this point had lost their cohesion. More recent examples of defence in depth include the multiple lines of trenches of the First World War, plans for the defence of Britain under threat of German invasion.

During the Battle of Normandy, Wehrmacht forces utilized the bocage of the area to create successive lines of defences to slow the attacking Allies in hopes that reinforcements would arrive. The Pacific Front also had many examples of Defence in Depth where the Japanese inflicted heavy casualties on the Americans in battles such as Tarawa, Saipan, Peleliu, Iwo Jima, and Okinawa.

As already mentioned, the term defence in depth is now used in many non-military contexts. For example, a defence in depth strategy to fire prevention does not focus all the resources only on the prevention of a fire; instead, it also requires the deployment of fire alarms, extinguishers, evacuation plans, mobile rescue and fire-fighting equipment and even nation-wide plans for deploying massive resources to a major blaze. Defence in depth may mean engineering which emphasizes redundancy - a system that keeps working when a component fails - over attempts to design components that will not fail in the first place. For example, an aircraft with four engines will be less likely to suffer total engine failure than a single-engined aircraft no matter how much effort goes into making the single engine reliable.

In nuclear engineering and nuclear safety, defence in depth denotes the practice of having multiple, redundant, and independent layers of safety systems for the single, critical point of failure: the reactor core. This helps to reduce the risk that a single failure of a critical system could cause a core meltdown or a catastrophic failure of reactor containment.

Likewise, in information security defense in depth represents the use of multiple computer security techniques to help mitigate the risk of one component of the defense being compromised or circumvented. An example could be anti-virus software installed on individual workstations when there is already virus protection on the firewalls and servers within the same environment.

Different security products from multiple vendors may be deployed to defend different potential vectors within the network, helping prevent a shortfall in any one defense leading to a wider failure.

GENEVA CENTRE FOR SECURITY POLICY

The Geneva Centre for Security Policy (GCSP) is an international foundation that was established in 1995 under Swiss law to "promote the building and maintenance of peace, security and stability". The GCSP was founded by the Swiss Federal Department of Defence, Civil Protection and Sport, in cooperation with the Federal Department of Foreign Affairs, as a Swiss contribution to Partnership for Peace (PfP).

Main Activities

It is apt to mention that the GCSP's core activity is the provision of expert training in comprehensive international peace and security policy for mid-career diplomats, military officers, and civil servants from foreign, defence, and other relevant ministries, as well as from international organisations. Participants in GCSP courses come from countries of the Euro-Atlantic Partnership Council, NATO's Mediterranean Dialogue, the Istanbul Cooperation Initiative, and beyond, including South and East Asia and Africa. In addition to its three principal courses (each lasting from three to nine months) offered in Geneva, the GCSP also offers tailor-made courses in Geneva, Brussels, New York, and other locations. Alumni from GCSP courses remain engaged in the Centre's activities.

GCSP faculty and senior staff, both academics and practitioners, come from a wide range of countries, disciplines, and interests, covering a broad spectrum of the security-policy arena. They write extensively in GCSP publications, internationally reputed peer-reviewed journals, and other publications. In addition, they contribute regularly to the policy and academic debates on key security issues. Moreover, the GCSP convenes conferences, workshops, and discussions to promote dialogue on peace and security issues. Some of the latter activities aim to facilitate discreet dialogue in post-conflict situations.

It is remarkable that the GCSP's activities focus on the following thematic areas:

- International Security
- Euro-Atlantic Security
- New Issues in Security
- Civil-Military Relations
- Conflict and Peacebuilding
- Geopolitics of Globalisation and Transnational Security
- Security and Law.

The GCSP's governing body is the Foundation Council, which consists of representatives of over 40 member states and the Canton of Geneva. GCSP management is guided on key policy issues by an international Advisory Board, which includes prominent persons with experience in the security field and in international organisations, government, civil society, and academia.

In fact, the Swiss government is the principal contributor to the GCSP's budget. Other Foundation Council members, partner states, and institutions·also support the GCSP by seconding faculty, funding scholarships, and contributing to other aspects of the Centre's activities.

REFERENCES

Amos Tversky / Daniel Kahneman, 1981. "The Framing of Decisions and the Psychology of Choice."

Apicella C. L. and all. Testosterone and financial risk preferences. Evolution and Human Behavior. Vol 29. Issue 6. 384-390.abstract.

Bankoff, Greg, George Frerks and Dorothea Hilhorst. 2004. *Mapping Vulnerability*. Sterling: Earthscan.

Birkmann, Joern (editor). 2006. *Measuring Vulnerability to Natural Hazards – Towards Disaster Resilient Societies*. UNU Press.

Cortada, James W. (2003-12-04) *The Digital Hand: How Computers Changed the Work of American Manufacturing, Transportation, and Retail Industries* USA: Oxford University Press pp. 512.

Cortada, James W. (2005-11-03) *The Digital Hand: Volume II: How Computers Changed the Work of American Financial, Telecommunicati ons, Media, and Entertainment Industries* USA: Oxford University Press.

Cortada, James W. (2007-11-06) *The Digital Hand, Vol 3: How Computers Changed the Work of American Public Sector Industries* USA: Oxford University Press, p. 496.

Damodaran, Aswath (2003). *Investment Philosophies: Successful Investment Philosophies and the Greatest Investors Who Made Them Work*. Wiley. p. 15.

Douglas Hubbard "The Failure of Risk Management: Why It's Broken and How to Fix It, John Wiley & Sons, 2009.

Drake, R. A. (2004). Selective potentiation of proximal processes: Neurobiological mechanisms for spread of activation. Medical Science Monitor, 10, 231-234.

Flyvbjerg, B., 2008, "Curbing Optimism Bias and Strategic Misrepresentation in Planning: Reference Class Forecasting in Practice." European Planning Studies, vol. 16, no. 1, January, pp. 3-21.

Frank Hyneman Knight "Risk, uncertainty and profit" pg. 19, Hart, Schaffner, and Marx Prize Essays, no. 31. Boston and New York: Houghton Mifflin. 1921.

James Franklin, 2001: *The Science of Conjecture: Evidence and Probability Before Pascal*, Baltimore: Johns Hopkins University Press, 274.

Landsburg, Steven (2003-03-03). "Is your life worth $10 million?". *Everyday Economics* (Slate). http://www.slate.com/id/2079475/ . Retrieved 2008-03-17.

McElroy, T., & Seta, J. J. (2004). On the other hand am I rational? Hemisphere activation and the framing effect. *Brain and Cognition,* 55, 572-580.

Sapienza P., Zingales L. and Maestripieri D. 2009. Gender differences in financial risk aversion and career choices are affected by testosterone. Proceedings of the National Academy of Sciences.

Schatz, J., Craft, S., Koby, M., & DeBaun, M. R. (2004). Asymmetries in visual-spatial processing following childhood stroke. Neuropsychology, 18, 340-352.

Thywissen, Katharina. 2006. "Components of Risk: A comparative glossary." SOURCE No. 2/2006. Bonn, Germany.

Villagran, Juan Carlos. ""Vulnerability: A conceptual and methodological review." SOURCE. No. 2/2006. Bonn, Germany.

Volberg, G., & Hubner, R. (2004). On the role of response conflicts and stimulus position for hemispheric differences in global/ local processing: An ERP study. *Neuropsychologia,* 42, 1805-1813.

2

Global Security: Concepts and Prospects

> "People always get tired of one another. I grow tired of myself whenever I am left alone for ten minutes, and I am certain that I am fonder of myself than anyone can be of another person."
>
> —*George Bernard Shaw*

In the preceding chapter we have put light on security and relevant issues.

In this chapter we intend to elucidate security from the viewpoint of military and strategy. Basic concepts and other notions of military security are given elaborate treatment. The discussion is supported by UN General Assembly's special reports.

It is pertinent to note that, basically, security is a condition in which States consider that there is no danger of military attack, political pressure or economic coercion, so that they are able to pursue freely their own development and progress. International security is thus the result and the sum of the security of each and every State member of the international community; accordingly, international security cannot be reached without full international co-operation.

However, security is a relative rather than an absolute term. National and international security need to be viewed as matters of degree.

It is apt to mention that study of security concepts and policies arises from several major developments in international relations. Force continues to be widely used as a means of promoting national security. Developments in science and technology and military strategy are driving the arms race, particularly in the nuclear field, to new heights and are thus increasing the dangers of nuclear war. New weapons By-stems and technologies, such as anti-satellite systems, laser and particle-beam weapons and long-range cruise missiles are significantly altering the composition of the military relationships among the major Powers.

Besides, the international diffusion of advanced military technologies and military capabilities is exacerbating the dangers of international conflicts. Meanwhile, the process of negotiation on measures of arms limitation and disarmament has so far achieved very little and lagged far behind arms technology developments. Issues relating to international peace and security are prominent among matters dealt with in various organs of the United Nations, such as the Security Council, the General Assembly both in its regular sessions and in special sessions devoted to disarmament, in subsidiary bodies of the Assembly, particularly the First Committee and the Disarmament Commission, as well as in the Conference on Disarmament at Geneva.

Through the years the General Assembly of the United Nations has adopted by consensus a number of documents on this important subject. In addition to various deliberations on the question of international peace and security within the United Nations framework, a series of expert studies, carried out by the Secretary-General with the assistance of qualified experts, has further demonstrated the efforts of the united Nations devoted to this important subject.

Remarkably, besides these worsening military developments, there are serious new challenges to global political and economic problems. The emergence of new centres of political and economic power, resource scarcities, trade deficits, financial debts, over-population and threats posed by natural calamities and environmental degradation have combined to create hitherto unforeseen problems in the period following the World War II. New actors, new issues, more complicated linkages between old issues all tug at the fabric of international relations. These circumstances challenge the capacity of the international community to adapt to the rapidity of global change and indeed create growing challenges in all aspects of human activities.

As pointed out by the Secretary-General, they have placed the world on the thin margin between catastrophe and survival. The shadow of nuclear war has given a historically unprecedented and urgent dimension to the concerns for global security.

It is pertinent to note that if the current situation is filled with danger, it is also filled with opportunity. At the very time when the consequences of nuclear war and the dangers of instability are greater than ever, so also are the potential rewards of co-operation and mutual understanding. Thus, the conditions that pose new threats also provide the incentive to search for new means of attaining security, new efforts to build a more stable world capable of accommodating global change peacefully, achieving arms reduction and disarmament, enhancing respect for sovereignty and human rights, and solving economic problems.

In fact, one nation's security is often another's insecurity, and between such diverging perceptions there is often little room for compromise and negotiation. Against the range of perceived threats and vulnerabilities that enter into the calculations of those entrusted with the safety and prosperity of individual nations, the logic of co-operation and accommodation often counts for little.

As alreacy mentioned, concepts of security are the different bases on which States and the International community as a whole rely for their security. Examples of concepts are the "balance of power", "deterrence," "peaceful coexistence" and "collective security." Security policies, on the other hand, are means to promote security, such as disarmament and arms limitation arrangement or the maintenance and development of military capabilities.

There is no clear-cut line between a "concept" and a "policy" and it is not necessary to define one as long as the general thrust is kept in mind. Any discussion of security concepts is complex and, understandably, controversial. It concerns important and sensitive political issues. The perspectives differ. Even the most basic definitions and perceptions may be subject to controversy.

Nevertheless, the need to discuss these issues is real if mutual trust, respect and understanding are to be enhanced. This discussion should take place on the broadest possible basis. No nation should withdraw from this challenge, but contribute to efforts that seek to identify the common ground between nations. This endeavours to give an overview of various security concepts and approaches through which States have striven to maximize their national security.

In this context the relationship of such concepts, policies and principles to the broader issues of international security will also be considered.

Issue of Balance of Power

It is apt to mention here that the "balance of power" has been a feature of international relations since the advent of the state system. Although the meaning of the term "balance of power" appears self-evident, it may be understood in several ways.

It may describe the general character of an international system where States, in the absence of a higher authority regulating relations between them, seek security by creating power arrangements that reduce the risk of attack upon them, a process that has tended to produce offsetting coalitions against emerging concentrations of power anywhere in the system. It may refer to a situation in which equivalent power is held by two or more nations or groups of nations and to a policy of promoting the creation or preservation of such equivalence in power. Also, it is sometimes understood as a system of international relations in which agreed arrangements are made by States concerning the operation and adjustment of their power relationships, which may be reflected either in a lower or higher level of armaments. The concept of balance of power had its heyday in the eighteenth and nineteenth centuries. In Europe, the concept was expressed as a multiple balance among at least five great Powers, any combination of which was considered capable of neutralizing an aggressor.

The system had no central organization. However, the concept suffered disrepute during the first half of the twentieth century. Various problems are inherent in the balance of power concept. In addition to the difficulty of defining and measuring "power", the concept implicitly legitimizes the use of force in international relations.

Furthermore, in their pursuit of security States often try to create and maintain a "favourable" balance of power, i.e. a preponderance of power for themselves, which adds to international tension and stimulates arms races. The balance of power as a system was not capable of dealing with the security needs of all States.

It often produced equilibrium between the great Powers but tolerated both territorial annexations in Europe and imperial expansion in regions of developing countries. The relative balance between countries in a region is a factor that States consider in addressing their security concerns. The perspective of a small and weak State is different from that of a major Power, and also depends on whether the State is a member of an alliance or not. Major powers can influence and upset the balance, while, very often, small nations do not have many options but to adjust to the situation and to try to stay out of the struggle for power and influence as best they can. Often they have become the victims of the power struggle and of situations when the balance is upset.

It must be remembered that the balance of power concept has often been the basis for the formation of military alliances. However, the various alliances that have been formed in the years since the World War II have been the product of a range of causes. In existing international conditions, a number of States, including many smaller and less powerful ones, see substantial value in arrangements with other countries for the provision of mutual assistance in the event of an armed attack against any of them.

In fact, the roots of the present arms race are many and complex. To a large extent they can be found in political and socio-economic differences between the countries from the two groups of States that later came to form the two main alliances. In political terms, the tensions between

East and West still constitute the central feature of the present arms race. The post-war alliance system has not been able to eliminate the essential dilemma of security in the nuclear age: the problem of ensuring mutual security. Any measure designed to improve the military security of one side may weaken the security of the other.

The post-war alliances have been able to increase their collective military strength but not to solve the problem of insecurity in the international system, especially in the nuclear age. States members of the Warsaw Treaty have proposed on various occasions the simultaneous dissolution of their alliance and the North Atlantic Treaty Organization (NATO), and, as a first step, their military organizations.

Deterrence: Concept and Issues

Basically, deterrence is a security concept whose objective is to dissuade a potential adversary from initiating war, by threatening the use of force in order either to deny an adversary from gaining his objectives by military means or to punish the adversary should he seek to do so.

In effect it seeks to persuade an adversary that the risks and costs of acts of aggression will exceed any gains that might be obtained from such acts. If war is not avoided, deterrence has failed.

Coming history, deterrence has probably been practised since the earliest stages of human existence. Although the concept of deterrence is not supported by all the major Powers or for that matter by various other countries, it remains an important concept because, with the proliferation of nuclear weapons and the growth in the size and destructive capacities of arsenals of conventional weapons, the pursuit of national policies designed to sustain deterrence inevitably has major implications for other countries and for broad international security.

In fact, in the view of some States, conventional deterrence depends for its effectiveness primarily on the possession by States of military capabilities that are structured for self-defence of their national territory, so as to deny an adversary the prospect of securing territorial, political or economic gains by the use of military force. In their view nuclear deterrence, in contrast, relies mainly on the possession of offensive nuclear capabilities that would be used to punish an adversary in the event that that adversary were to initiate conflict. Some of them consider that some additional capabilities may also be needed, such as those that would enable retaliatory attacks to be conducted against military installations in an aggressor State's own territory. In the view of some other States, conventional deterrence is based on the same negative features as nuclear deterrence. They consider that the creation of highly precise weapons of great destructive power on the basis of the most modern technology, which in their destructive capacity approach nuclear weapons, lead to lowering the threshold between conventional and nuclear deterrence; the plans providing for the use of such weapons by a nuclear weapon State or by its ally against targets in the territory of a presumed adversary would lower the "nuclear threshold" and would inevitably increase the risk of nuclear war.

It must be remembered that a distinction that can be made between conventional and nuclear deterrence relates to their consequences, should deterrence fail and conflict eventuate. Although failures in conventional deterrence could well result in wars causing enormous devastation, failure of nuclear deterrence would threaten the very survival of humankind.

As the possibility that nuclear deterrence might fail cannot be ruled out, the viability and implications of this concept of security are of major concern to all. The notions of "balance" and "parity" play an important role in the relationship between East and West and in nuclear deterrence. However, these terms are interpreted in different ways.

Sometimes the "balance" is calculated on the level of a region or on the level of specific weapon systems. Sometimes it is interpreted on the global level, taking into account conventional and nuclear forces and allowing for the wide difference in the structure of deployed weapons. "Parity" is sometimes defined as a situation when neither side possesses the capacity for a "disarming" nuclear missile strike; if either side became the victim of nuclear aggression it would preserve sufficient means to deal a retaliating blow to the aggressor. It can also, however, refer to quantitative and qualitative aspects of the nuclear arsenals of the two sides.

In the similar vein, the concept of nuclear deterrence is subject to great controversy. In the following paragraphs an attempt is made to summarize the differing views on this concept. Some States that are proponents of nuclear deterrence consider that possession of a capability to retaliate with nuclear weapons has been and is likely to remain a virtual guarantee preventing the outbreak of any major conflict - either conventional or nuclear - among the nuclear-weapon States. They argue that the prospect of mutual devastation that each would suffer from nuclear conflict gives all concerned a fundamental interest in the avoidance of war.

They note in this regard the absence of armed conflict in Europe or between the United States and the Soviet Union for 40 years as *prima facie* evidence of the effectiveness of nuclear deterrence as a means of preserving peace. Decisions to acquire nuclear weapons are justified with what they perceive as requirements to deter war. It is central to the concept of deterrence that force would be used only in response to an attack by an adversary.

Furthermore, the proponents argue that nuclear deterrence serves not only to deter war but also to compel both sides to seek to avoid situations in which their vital interests may become directly opposed. Many opponents of the concept of deterrence reject the concept out of hand. They challenge its basic assumptions. In their view, the doctrine of deterrence is by nature aggressive and relies on force and provides a basis for an unrestricted arms race, particularly the nuclear arms race. They argue that the nuclear deterrence policy pursued by some States ranks first in their approach to agreements on disarmament, especially to a comprehensive test ban treaty, a nuclear weapon freeze and non-first-use of nuclear weapons.

Furthermore, they hold the view that it also feeds the arms spiral in the conventional field and firmly believe that deterrence objectively leads to a higher risk of nuclear war and more tensions in international relations. This concept of security, they conclude, entails an unprecedented threat to human survival.

Some other States, regard it as being the only reliable arrangement against nuclear war at present in operation. Pending the development of effective collective security arrangements and major reductions in nuclear arms, these States consider that it is important to assist in the maintenance of the system of nuclear deterrence because of the importance of the contribution they consider it makes to international stability.

Without such stability, they consider that arms reduction agreements and progress toward effective collective security arrangements would be impossible. Many other States, which do not possess nuclear weapons, may accept conventional deterrence as a means for achieving national security but have serious doubts about the concept of nuclear deterrence. As long as nuclear weapons exist national security planners must develop concepts to guide decisions on -nuclear weapons. These States are of the opinion that nuclear weapons do not serve any military purpose and that as long as nuclear disarmament is not achieved, any nuclear weapons concept must assure the avoidance of nuclear war.

These States question the capability of the concept of nuclear deterrence to serve this purpose in the long-term perspective. For one thing, they argue that nuclear deterrence cannot be made foolproof. The doctrine provides no guarantee against irrational human behaviour or the malfunctioning of command and control systems. They further challenge the proposition that the absence of nuclear war so far can be attributed to nuclear deterrence.

They also believe that nuclear deterrence has not prevented intervention by great Powers in developing countries and may have served to disperse great Power conflicts to these developing areas. In their view the arguments about the peace-keeping effects of nuclear deterrence may influence decisions regarding possible acquisition of nuclear weapons of non-nuclear-weapon States and have a negative influence on the non-proliferation regime. They believe that the stability of nuclear deterrence is constantly threatened by technological advances.

The concept, implies a complacency with nuclear weapons and more and more serves to vindicate decisions to expand nuclear weapons programmes; nuclear deterrence has not been conducive to reductions in armaments. They feel that inherent in the concept is a strong element of offensive threat and mutual insecurity that breeds suspicion and fear; this hampers efforts to build confidence and reduce tensions between States. The present level of nuclear arsenals, all but a fraction of which is in the hands of the two leading military Powers, is enough to destroy human civilization.

Notwithstanding the differences in the nuclear weapons policies of the States that possess such weapons, the fact remains that in certain circumstances they may be used. No nuclear-weapon State has completely renounced the possibility of their use. Any use of nuclear weapons is at the same time a threat against all mankind.

Nuclear warfare, if it were to occur, would have consequences affecting not only the nuclear-weapon States and their allies. The assured destruction would not be mutual between the adversaries, but global. Among the non-nuclear-weapon States there is therefore a growing sense of insecurity and of loss of their right to determine their own destiny.

Equal Security

It is apt to mention that equal security is not a security concept but a principle for bilateral arms negotiations that parties may agree upon. For example, in a joint communique issued on 29 May 1972 the United States and the Soviet Union declared their intentions to limit strategic offensive arms "and to conduct them [their negotiations] in a spirit of goodwill, respect for each other's legitimate interests and observance of the principle of equal security." This principle would seem to embrace the notion that neither State has the right to claim exclusivity or to demand for itself any special privileges or advantages.

Indeed, it has been stated that mutual security between the two major nuclear-weapon States can only be assured by equality. However, questions have been raised as to its exact meaning and wider applicability.

Critics maintain that this principle does not address the security concerns of medium-sized and small States, particularly in the light of the wide disparities in military capabilities that exist in the world of present time.

Collective Security

In fact, the concept of collective security is based on a global commitment to international peace and security undertaken as a legal obligation of all nations. It is the first attempt to institutionalize and enforce the rule of international law to enhance the security of all nations. The international community, acting together, is committed to move promptly to encounter any act of aggression by one nation against another.

It is remarkable to note here that collective security implies an acknowledgement that security is indivisible. It provides protection of national interests and sovereignty in a collective manner and leads to the strengthening of international security. As a concept it aims at a broader objective than just the absence of war by taking into account the wider requirements of international peace and security.

It is based on renunciation of force, except in self-defence, commitment to the peaceful settlement of international disputes and obligation to support collective measures, both military and non-military, to defeat aggression. A major problem with the concept of collective security is that on a number of occasions States have been reluctant to fulfil their obligations, which is the basic condition for the functioning of the system.

In the case of the League of Nations this lack of political will was aggravated by the absence of an effective enforcement mechanism and by the lack of universality in the League. Within the United Nations special voting powers have been accorded to five States as permanent members of the Security Council. Collective security action by the United Nations requires the concurrence of the five permanent members of the Council: a negative vote by any one of the five States "vetoes" the proposed action. However, the "veto" provision reflects the original assumption that the great Powers would maintain a co-operative working relationship among themselves and, therefore, only use the veto in exceptional circumstances.

In practice disagreements between the permanent members have in a number of cases led to the use of the veto, which, in turn, has prevented collective security action. The view has been expressed that the veto power has been abused.

Concept of Neutrality

Basically, the policy of neutrality practised by a few, mainly European, countries is one such policy. Historically a function of great Power relations and armed hostilities in Europe, it has currently evolved in response to the East-West conflict. In strict usage, the term neutrality is applicable only in times of war, indicating the legal status of a State that has declared itself neutral in relation to the belligerents during armed hostilities.

The rights and obligations of neutrals in times of war are laid down in international law. In order to remain neutral in war a State abstains from participation in the war efforts of the belligerents. In a war situation, the Hague Conventions of 1907 and 1912 have to be taken into account. As long as a State acts in accordance with the international rules on neutrality, international law safeguards the status of neutrality.

There are no rules of international law concerning how a neutral State must act in peace-time. Neutral States are thus not required to refrain from taking a position on political, economic or social issues facing the international community. Neutrality in war and policies during peace-time are necessarily connected. In some instances, neutrality has been confirmed by international guarantees or reinforced through constitutional arrangements.

Most importantly, the neutral States avoid such peace-time commitments as might jeopardize the possibility of upholding neutrality in war-time and therefore do not participate in military alliances. Also in other respects a policy is pursued that inspires and sustains the confidence in the determination and ability to remain neutral and independent in war-time. The pursuit of a policy of neutrality aims at ensuring the security of neutral countries in accordance with their national interests. One basic characteristic of a security policy based on neutrality is that it is not offensive.

The military forces of neutral countries are designed to make credible the commitment to uphold their neutral status in war. Because of their independence from military alliances neutral States have been able to contribute substantially to reducing international tensions and antagonisms in their regions and on a larger scale. Through the United Nations, the Conference on Security and Co-operation in Europe and other international forums, neutral States have taken an active part in the processes of co-operation, mediation and peace-keeping.

Non-alignment Movement

It is apt to mention that Non-alignment (now almost passive) is not merely a policy of Governments but also a movement of the peoples of non-aligned countries. A number of newly independent nations emerged in the post-war era. During the same period the power and rivalry of military alliances also increased. In this climate of the cold war, it was only natural that non-aligned nations should get together to protect themselves from its consequences. They did not wish to take sides in a conflict from which they had little to gain and much to lose. The realization of this common danger, which was nothing short of a danger to their newly won independence, persuaded them to co-ordinate their perceptions and policies on a more regular basis.

Non-alignment may be seen as a response not only to the cold war that characterized the period after the World War II, but also to the challenges of the process of decolonization, especially in Africa. It has reacted against the dangers inherent in great Power struggles, military alliances and the arms race, voiced its opposition to colonialism and expressed a reaffirmation of the principle of the equality of all nations in the international system. The Bandung Conference of Asian and African countries, held at Bandung, Indonesia, in 1955, was an important milestone in Afro-Asian history and some of the ideas were later taken up by non-aligned nations. In developing the concept of non-alignment, a number of political leaders from the countries concerned made a considerable contribution to this concept. Following are the basic elements:

(a) staying out of military blocs or other forms of great Power entanglements;

(b) working towards defusing international tensions and promoting peace;

(c) peaceful coexistence and peaceful co-operation among States irrespective of their social or political systems;

(d) support for people struggling for freedom from colonialism, opposition to racism, *apartheid,* etc.;

(e) support for disarmament, especially nuclear disarmament;

(f) working towards a more just and equitable international order. These elements formed the core of the non-aligned policies in the 1950s and 1960s and constituted rallying posts for etire gamut of the non-aligned movement.

The first Conference of Heads of State or Government of Non-Aligned Countries was held in Belgrade, Yugoslavia, in 1961, with 25 countries participating and 3 countries represented by observers. At the Belgrade Conference, a number of issues related to international peace and security as well as social and economic development were considered, particularly the questions of nuclear disarmament and a nuclear test ban. The appeal of non-aligned countries on the nuclear test ban made an important contribution to the conclusion of the partial test ban treaty of 1963.

The Heads of State or Government of participating countries adopted a declaration that upheld the following principles: (a) a new world order should be based on co-operation between nations and founded on freedom, equality and social justice for the promotion of prosperity; (b) lasting peace can be achieved only if the domination of colonialism-imperialism and neo-colonialism in all their manifestations is radically eliminated; (c) to eradicate the source of conflict threatening world peace nations should accept and practise a policy of peaceful coexistence in the world; (d) all peoples and nations have to solve the problems of their own political, economic, social and cultural systems in accordance with their own conditions, needs and potentialities; (e) peoples and Governments shall refrain from any use of ideologies for the purpose of waging cold war, exercising pressure or imposing their will. In addition, they stated that non-aligned countries "do not wish to form a new bloc and cannot be a bloc" and considered that "under present conditions, the existence and the activities of non-aligned countries in the interests of peace are one of the more important factors for safeguarding world peace."

These principles laid down in the Belgrade and subsequent conferences have constituted the basic platform of the non-aligned movement. At the same time, there have been some] adjustments in accordance with changing international situations during the past decades. For instance, the second summit, in 1964 in Cairo, put forward a programme for peace and international co-operation and focused attention on the as yet unfinished struggle for the liberation of Africa.

These ideas were carried a step forward at the 1970 Lusaka summit where focus was placed on peace, independence, development, co-operation and democratization of international relations. Apart from giving greater attention to economic issues, the Lusaka summit made an appeal for the creation of a zone of peace in the Indian Ocean.

It also helped consolidate the non-aligned position on the law of the sea issue at the United Nations. The Algiers summit in 1973 laid stress on making detente a wider concept, applicable to all parts of the world, and not confined to a particular region. The Colombo summit in 1976 called for the preservation of the essential character of non-alignment and the strengthening (of its resistance to politics of pressure, and rejected the notions of an international order based on power blocs, balance of power and spheres of influence. The Havana summit in 1979 confirmed the concept of non-alignment and called for global negotiations for the new international economic order. A unique feature of this summit was the special attention given to issues in Latin America and the Caribbean.

The New Delhi summit in 1983 particularly underlined the importance of peace, nuclear disarmament and development. For the past decades, the non-aligned countries have made considerable efforts and contributions to the question of nuclear disarmament both within and outside the framework of the United Nations.

In addition to the political aspect of non-alignment, the economic factor constituted one of the main motive forces and later became the strongest motive that impelled the non-aligned countries to co-operation and joint action. More recently, the movement has become a forum for promoting the new international economic order based on equity, co-operation and interdependence.

No doubt, Non-Aligned Movement has made several positive contributions to international security. Individual countries or groups of non-aligned nations have sought to help resolve specific conflicts among members of the Movement, as, for example, the Iran-Iraq war. The Movement has strengthened the independence of new nations by enhancing respect for their positions in international affairs. Moreover, it has provided an effective means of gaining collective weight in international forums to press for important issues of racial, political and economic justice.

Peaceful Coexistence

It is pertinent to note that ince the First World War, the concept of peaceful coexistence has been put forward as a fundamental norm in international relations. In the light of the complexity of the contemporary world, with some 160 independent countries of different peoples, language, culture, customs, ideology, political institutions and socio-economic systems, the idea of peaceful coexistence is designed to accommodate the perceivable conflicts and contending interests among States.

Peaceful coexistence is not intended to mean just passive coexistence, but also active co-operation and understanding among all States on the basis of equality and mutual benefit. Furthermore, it could also be regarded as an effective and practical contribution to confidence-building among nations. In the opinion of its proponents, peaceful coexistence applies universally to all States regardless of their size, international status or political and socio-economic systems.

They also underline that the threats and problems mankind is facing now, in the nuclear age, make it a matter of extraordinary importance that all States meet the demands inherent in the principles of peaceful coexistence; this would be an important contribution to the strengthening of international security.

Common Security

Basically, the idea of common security was put forward in the report of the Independent Commission on Disarmament and Security Issues (A/CN. 10/38 and Corr.1) . The Commission stated that "a doctrine of common security must replace the present expedient of deterrence through armaments. International peace must rest on a commitment to joint survival rather than a threat of mutual destruction". The Independent Commission on Disarmament and Security Issues convened with the purpose of finding new ways of thinking about and organizing for security in response to the failure of mutual deterrence to lessen international insecurities.

The Commission began with the premise that threats to security - the conventional and nuclear arms races, resource shortages, environmental degradation, underdevelopment - are threats that nations increasingly have in common, and that solutions should therefore be sought in common.

As the Commission reported, the key to security lies in the willingness of nations to organize their security policies in co-operation with each other. The Commission recommended that the process of co-operation begin with relations between the Soviet Union and the United States and their respective alliance systems, in particular, with negotiations over conventional and nuclear arms limitation and with policies to encourage *rapprochement* and normalization of relations between the super-Powers.

The objective of these efforts, the Commission noted, should be the re-establishment of peaceful relations, policies of restraint, reversal of the arms race and the implementation of confidence-building measures between the Soviet Union and the United States. The Commission also proposed that the search for co-operative solutions should include the developing countries, which share the risks and therefore the responsibilities for peace. The Commission recommended measures to mitigate the circumstances that feed conflict and crisis in the developing countries and pose in threats of great Power involvement.

In particular, the Commission addressed the problem of underdevelopment, which fuels the discontent that leads to expending arms budgets, civil conflict and international expanding international destabilization and war.

It is apt to mention that the concept of common security has relevance first of all to the relationship between the nuclear alliances in general and to the relation between the Soviet Union and the United States in particular. Common security is a recognition of the fact that nuclear weapons have changed not only the scale of warfare but the very concept of war itself. In the nuclear age war cannot be an instrument of policy. A nuclear war would have no winners, only losers. There is no defence against nuclear weapons.

The only protection against nuclear destruction is the avoidance of nuclear war itself. Even ideological opponents have a shared interest in survival and, thus, in the avoidance of war. Common security as a concept is based on two preferences: for international over national means of achieving security; and for means that are peaceful over those that rely on the use or the threatened use of force. These extremely venerable preferences are interpreted in the light of modern destructive technologies, principally nuclear but also "conventional", chemical and biological weapons.

On the other hand, the existence of modern weapons makes it likely that the costs of resorting to military force (certainly to nuclear force) would exceed the benefits; no one would win a nuclear war. On the other hand, the effects of the use of modern weapons would cross international frontiers. No country would be secure from the consequences of nuclear war: "national" and "international" interests coincide in the need to prevent war. The notion of common security is founded on the assumption that in an age of interdependence no nation can find security by itself.

Thus, the goal of common security is to begin a positive process that will eventually lead to peace and disarmament, and that will tap the recent outpouring of popular concern over the dangers of war. The results of this process would be a safer, more secure international order: a world with no nuclear weapons, with peace and security maintained at lower levels of conventional arms, and with increased national and international resources reallocated to the purpose of improving the quality of life.

Obviously, the information furnished in the preceding paragraphs may have enlightened you to understand the basic concepts of military security. In fact in the rapidly changing world order, many new security equations may arise and lose meaning in course of time. NAM is such an case.

Now we turn to the issue of national security.

3

National Security: Concept and Issues

> "A nation has security when it does not have to sacrifice its legitimate interests to avoid war, and is able, if challenged, to maintain them by war."
>
> —*Walter Lippmann*

In simple terms, by national security we mean the requirement to maintain the survival of the nation-state through the use of economic, military and political power and the exercise of diplomacy. The concept developed mostly in the United States of America after World War II. Initially focusing on military might, it now encompasses a broad range of facets, all of which impinge on the military or economic security of the nation and the values espoused by the national society.

Accordingly, in order to possess national security, a nation needs to possess economic security, energy security, environmental security, etc. Security threats involve not only conventional foes such as nation-states but also non-state actors such as terrorist organizations, narcotic cartels and multi-national organizations; some authorities including natural disasters and events causing severe environmental damage in this category.

There is no single universally accepted definition of "National Security". A typical dictionary definition, in this case from Farlex dictionary, defines national security as the following:

> "the requirement to maintain the survival of the nation-state through the use of economic, military and political power and the exercise of diplomacy."

However, a variety of definitions provide an overview of the many usages of this concept. The concept still remains ambiguous, having originated from simpler definitions which initially emphasised the freedom from military threat and political coercion to later increase in sophistication and include other forms of non-military security as suited the circumstances of the time.

Measures taken to ensure national security include:

- using diplomacy to rally allies and isolate threats
- marshalling economic power to facilitate or compel cooperation
- maintaining effective armed forces
- implementing civil defense and emergency preparedness measures (including anti-terrorism legislation)
- ensuring the resilience and redundancy of critical infrastructure
- using intelligence services to detect and defeat or avoid threats and espionage, and to protect classified information
- using counterintelligence services or secret police to protect the nation from internal threats

Harold Lasswell, a political scientist, in 1950, looks at national security from almost the same aspect, that of external coercion:

> "The distinctive meaning of national security means freedom from foreign dictation."

The 1996 definition propagated by the National Defence College of India resembles the accretion of the elements of national power:

> "National security is an appropriate and aggressive blend of political resilience and maturity, human resources, economic structure and capacity, technological competence, industrial base and availability of natural resources and finally the military might."

Arnold Wolfers (1960), while recognising the need to segregate the subjectivity of the conceptual idea from the objectivity, talks of threats to *acquired values*:

> "An ambiguous symbol meaning different things to different people. National security objectively means the absence of threats to acquired values and subjectively, the absence of fear that such values will be attacked."

The United States Armed Forces defines national security (of the United States) in the following manner :

> National security — A collective term encompassing both national defense and foreign relations of the United States. Specifically, the condition provided by: a. a military or defense advantage over any foreign nation or group of nations; b. a favorable foreign relations position; or c. a defense posture capable of successfully resisting hostile or destructive action from within or without, overt or covert.

Harold Brown, U.S. Secretary of Defense (1977 to 1981), defined national security in his 1983 book *Thinking about national security: defense and foreign policy in a dangerous world*. The definition includes elements such as economic security and environmental security.

> "National security then is the ability to preserve the nation's physical integrity and territory; to maintain its economic relations with the rest of the world on reasonable terms;

> to preserve its nature, institution, and governance from disruption from outside; and to control its borders."

In the words of Charles Maier:

> "National security... is best described as a capacity to control those domestic and foreign conditions that the public opinion of a given community believes necessary to enjoy its own self-determination or autonomy, prosperity and wellbeing."

Barack Obama (2010) included an all-encompassing world-view in his definition of America's national security interests as:

- The security of the United States, its citizens, and U.S. allies and partners;
- A strong, innovative, and growing U.S. economy in an open international economic system that promotes opportunity and prosperity;
- Respect for universal values at home and around the world; and
- An international order advanced by U.S. leadership that promotes peace, security, and opportunity through stronger cooperation to meet global challenges.

Backdrop

It is apt to mention that the origin of the modern concept of "national security" as a philosophy of maintaining a stable nation state can be traced to the Peace of Westphalia, wherein the concept of a sovereign state, ruled by a sovereign, became the basis of a new international order of nation states. As an academic concept, national security can be seen as a recent phenomenon which was first introduced in the United States after World War II, and has to some degree replaced other concepts that describe the struggle of states to overcome various external and internal threats.

The earliest mention of the term national security, however, was made in Yale University in 1790 wherein reference was made to its relation with domestic industries. The concept of national security became an official guiding principle of foreign policy in the United States when the National Security Act of 1947 was signed on July 26, 1947 by U.S. President Harry S. Truman. Together with its 1949 amendment, this act created important facets for American national security such as the precursor to the Department of Defense), subordinated the military branches to the new cabinet level position of the Secretary of Defense, established the National Security Council and the Central Intelligence Agency.

The Act did not define national security which was conceivably advantageous as it's ambiguity made it a powerful phrase to invoke whenever issues threatened by other interests of the state, such as domestic concerns, came up for discussion and decision.

In fact, the realisation that national security encompasses more than just military security was present, though understated, from the beginning itself. The US National Security Act of 1947 was set up "to advise the President on the integration of domestic, military and foreign policies relating to national security".

In India, the Institute for Defence Studies and Analyses (IDSA) realised in 1965 that "national security is a wider concept than defence."

Gen Maxwell Taylor's essay of 1974 titled "The Legitimate Claims of National Security" has this to say:

> "The national valuables in this broad sense include current assets and national interests, as well as the sources of strength upon which our future as a nation depends. Some valuables are tangible and earthy; others are spiritual or

intellectual. They range widely from political assets such as the Bill of Rights, our political institutions and international friendships, to many economic assets which radiate worldwide from a highly productive domestic economy supported by rich natural resources. It is the urgent need to protect valuables such as these which legitimizes and makes essential the role of national security."

Main Elements

It is pertinent to note that as in the case of national power, the military aspect of security is an important, but not the sole, component of national security. To be truly secure, a nation needs other forms of security. Authorities differ in their choice of nation security elements. Besides the military aspect of security, the aspects of diplomacy or politics; society; environment; energy and natural resources; and economics are commonly listed.

The elements of national security corelate closely to the concept of the elements of national power. Romm (1993) lists security from narcotic cartels, economic security, environmental security and energy security as the non-military elements of national security.

Military Security

This is traditionally, the earliest recognised form of national security. Military security implies the capability of a nation to defend itself, and/or deter military aggression. Alternatively, military security implies the capability of a nation to enforce its policy choices by use of military force. The term "military security" is considered synonymous with "security" in much of its usage.

One of the definitions of security given in the *Dictionary of Military and Associated Terms*, may be considered a definition of "military security":

> "A condition that results from the establishment and maintenance of protective measures that ensure a state of inviolability from hostile acts or influences."

Political Security

The political aspect of security has been offered by Barry Buzan, Ole Wæver, Jaap de Wilde as an important component of national security, Political security is about the stability of the social order. Closely allied to military security and societal security, other components proposed in a framework for national security in their book "Security: a new framework for analysis", it specifically addresses threats to sovereignty. System referent objects are defined, such as nation-states, nations, transnational groups of political importance including tribes, minorities, some religious organisations, systems of states such as the European Union and the United Nations, besides others. Diplomacy, negotiation and other interactions form the means of interacion between the objects,

Economic Security

Historically, conquest of nations have made conquerors rich through plunder, access to new resources and enlarged trade through controlling of the conquered nations' economy. In today's complex system of international trade, characterised by multi-national agreements, mutual interdependence and availability of natural resources etc., the freedom to follow choice of policies to develop a nation's economy in the manner desired, forms the essence of economic security. Economic security today forms, arguably, as important a part of national security as military security.

Environmental Security

Environmental security deals with environmental issues which threaten the national security of a nation in any manner. The scope and nature of environmental threats to national security and strategies to engage them are a subject of debate. While all environmental events are not considered significant of being categorised as threats, many transnational issues, both global and regional would affect national security.

Romm (1993) classifies these as:

- *Transnational environmental problems that threaten a nation's security, in its broad defined sense.* These include global environmental problems such as climate change due to global warming, deforestation and loss of biodiversity, etc.
- *Environmental or resource problems that threaten a nation's security, traditionally defined.* These would be problems whose outcomes would result in conventional threats to national security as first or higher order outcomes. Such disputes could range from heightened tension or outright conflict due to disputes over water scarcity in the Middle East, to illegal immigration into the United States caused by the failure of agriculture in Mexico. The genocide in Rwanda,indirectly or partly caused by rise in population and dwindling availability of farmland, is an example of the extremity of outcome arising from problems of environmental security.
- *Environmentally threatening outcomes of warfare*, e.g. Romans destroyed the fields of Carthage by pouring salt over them; Saddam Hussein's burning of oil wells in the Gulf War; the use of Agent Orange by the USA in the Vietnam War for defoilating forests for military purposes.

Security of Energy and Natural Resources

A resource has been defined as:

> "...a support inventory... biotic or abiotic, renewable or expendable,... for sustaining life at a heightened level of well-being."
>
> —*Prabhakaran Paleri (2008)*

It is pertinent to note that resources include water, sources of energy, land and minerals. Availability of adequate natural resources is an important for a nation to develop its industry and economic power. Lack of resources is a serious challenge for Japan to overcome to increase its national power. In the Gulf War of 1990, fought over economic issues, Iraq captured Kuwait in order to capture its oil wells, among other reasons. Water resources are subject to disputes between many nations, including the two nuclear powers, India and Pakistan. Nations attempt to attain energy and natural resource security by acquiring the needed resources by force, negotiation and commerce.

Rights & Freedoms in Security Perspective

It is apt to mention that the measures adopted to maintain national security in the face of threats to society has led to ongoing dialectic, particularly in liberal democracies, on the appropriate scale and role of authority in matters of civil and human rights.

Remarkably, tension exists between the preservation of the state (by maintaining self-determination and sovereignty) and the rights and freedoms of individuals. Although national security measures are imposed to protect society as a whole, many such measures will restrict the rights and freedoms of all individuals in society. The concern is that where the exercise of national security laws and powers is not subject to good governance, the rule of law, and strict checks and balances, there is a risk that "national security" may simply serve as a pretext for suppressing unfavorable political and social views.

Taken to its logical conclusion, this view contends that measures which may ostensibly serve a national security purpose (such as mass surveillance, and censorship of mass media), could ultimately lead to an Orwellian dystopia. In the United States, the politically controversial USA Patriot Act and other government action has brought some of these issues to the citizen's attention, raising two main questions - to what extent, for the sake of national security, should individual rights and freedoms be restricted *and* can the restriction of civil rights for the sake of national security be justified?

Technical Aspects

It is apt to mention that because of the highly competitive nature of nation states, national security for countries with significant resources and value is based largely on technical measures and operational processes. This ranges from information protection related to state secrets to weaponry for militaries to negotiations strategies with other nation states.

The national security aparatus depends largely on combinations of management practices, technical capabilities, the projection of images both internally and externally, and the capacity to gain enough of the will of the people to gather taxes and spend them on useful efforts.

While some nation states use power to gain more power for their leadership, others provide quality of life improvements to their people, thus creating larger geopolitical conflicts between types of governments. These all have foundations in internal education and communications systems that serve to build the nation states on strategic and tactical bases and create the conditions for success and failure of the nation-state.

Increasingly the world is replacing transportation with communication and thus the ability to communicate effectively and convey messages in the information environment is critical to national security for the Western nations. Issues like global warming and research priorities increasingly dominate the reality of competition between nation states.

All of these lead to the need to have a clear understanding of the technical issues underlying national security in order to create and sustain the institutions that ultimately feed the future of the nation state.

REFERENCES

Davis, Robert T. (2010). Robert T. Davis. ed. *U.S. Foreign Policy and National Security: Chronology and Index for the 20th Century*. Praeger Security International Series (Illustrated ed.). ABC-CLIO. p. xiii=xiv.

Definition from "Proceedings of Seminar on "A Maritime Strategy for India" (1996). National Defence College, Tees January Marg, New Delhi, India. quoted in Paleri 2008 (ibid).

Diamond, Jared. "Malthus in Africa: Rwanda's Genocide". http://www.ditext.com/diamond/10.html. Retrieved 26 September 2010.

MacFarlane, S. Neil; Yuen Foong Khong (2006). S. Neil, MacFarlane; Yuen Foong Khong. eds. *Human security and the UN: a critical history*. United Nations intellectual history project (illustrated ed.). Indiana University Press, p. 346.

MAIER, CHARLES S. *Peace and security for the 1990s*.Unpublished paper for the MacArthur Fellowship Program, Social Science Research Council, 12 Jun 1990. As quoted in Romm 1993, p. 5.

Obama, Barack. *National Security Strategy, May 2010*. Office of the President of the United States, The White House. Accessed 23 September 2010.

Romm, Joseph J. (1993). *Defining national security: the nonmilitary aspects*. Pew Project on America's Task in a Changed World (Pew Project Series). Council on Foreign Relations, p. 122.

Security: a new framework for analysis. Lynne Rienner Publishers. 1998, p. 239.

Taylor, Gen Maxwell (1974). "The Legitimate Claims of National Security". *Foreign Affairs* (Council on Foreign Relations, Inc.) (Essay of 1974).

4

International Peace and Security

> "Discontent is the want of self-reliance: it is infirmity of will."
>
> —*Ralf Waldo Emerson*

First it is apt to mention that one of the primary purposes for establishing the United Nations — and a central part of its mandate — is the maintenance of international peace and security. Since its creation, the United Nations has been called upon many times to prevent the threat of conflict escalating into war, to persuade opposing parties to use the conference table rather than force of arms, or to help restore peace when conflict does break out.

Nodoubt, over the decades, the United Nations has successfully helped to end numerous conflicts, often through actions of the Security Council — the primary organ for dealing with international peace and security issues. The end of the cold war brought a time of hope and change and rising expectations for the United Nations, and Member States looked for ways to strengthen the Organization's capacity for preventive diplomacy, for peacemaking and for peacekeeping.

It must be remembered that to address a surge in intra-State conflicts, the Seecurity Council authorized innovative and complex peacekeeping operations. In El

Salvador and Guatemala, in Cambodia and in Mozambique, the United Nations played a major role in ending civil war and bringing peace. But recent conflicts, many of which have been characterized by ethnic violence, such as in Somalia, Rwanda and the former Yugoslavia, brought new challenges to the United Nations peacemaking role.

The current incessant civil war in Libya (Feb. 2011) and similar probable outburst in other Gulf countries and elsewhere (possibly in China) may pose serious threat before the world from peace and security perspective.

The United Nations system as a whole is focusing as never before on peace-building — action to support structures that will strengthen and consolidate peace. Experience has shown that keeping peace, in the sense of avoiding military conflict, is not sufficient for establishing a secure and lasting peace. Such security can only be achieved by helping countries to foster economic development, social justice, protection of human rights, good governance and the democratic process.

No other institution has the multilateral experience, competence, coordinating ability and impartiality that the United Nations brings to providing assistance in these tasks.

In fact, the Security Council, the General Assembly and the Secretary-General all play major, complementary roles in fostering peace and security. United Nations activities cover the principal areas of peacemaking, peacekeeping, enforcement and peace-building.

The Security Council

The Charter — an international treaty — obligates Member States to settle their disputes by peaceful means, in such a manner that international peace and security, and justice, are not endangered. They are to refrain from the threat or use of force against any State, and may bring any dispute before the Security Council.

The Security Council is the United Nations organ primarily responsible for maintaining peace and security. Under the Charter, Member States are obliged to accept and carry out the Council's decisions. Recommendations of other United Nations bodies do not have the mandatory force the decisions of the Security Council have, but can influence situations as they express the opinion of the international community.

When a dispute is brought to its attention, the Council's first action is usually to recommend to the parties to reach agreement by peaceful means. In some cases, the Council itself undertakes investigation and mediation. It may set forth principles for a peaceful settlement. It may appoint special representatives or ask the Secretary-General to use his good offices.

When a dispute leads to fighting, the Council's first concern is to bring it to an end as quickly as possible. The Council may issue ceasefire directives that can be instrumental in preventing wider hostilities. In support of a peace process, the Council may deploy military observers or a peacekeeping force to an area of conflict.

The Charter, the Council is empowered to take measures to enforce its decisions. It can impose embargoes and economic sanctions, or it can authorize the use of force to ensure that mandates are fulfilled.

In some cases, the Council has authorized, the use of military force by a coalition of Member States or by a regional organization or arrangement. But the Council takes such action only as a last resort, when peaceful means of settling a dispute have been exhausted, and after determining that a threat to the peace, a breach of the peace or act of aggression exists.

The Council has established international criminal tribunals to prosecute persons accused of serious violations of international humanitarian law, including genocide.

The General Assembly

The United Nations Charter empowers the General Assembly to "consider the general principles of cooperation in the maintenance of international peace and security" and "make recommendations ... to the Members or to the Security Council or to both". The Assembly offers a means for finding consensus on difficult issues, providing a forum for the airing of grievances and diplomatic exchanges. To foster the maintenance of peace, it has held special or emergency special sessions on issues such as disarmament, the question of Palestine or the situation in Afghanistan.

The General Assembly considers peace and security issues in its First (Disarmament and International Security) Committee and in its Fourth (Special Political and Decolonization) Committee.

Over the years, the Assembly has helped promote peaceful relations among nations by adopting declarations on peace, the peaceful settlement of disputes and international cooperation. The Assembly in 1980 approved the establishment in San Jose, Costa Rica, of the **University for Peace,** a specialized international institute for studies, research and dissemination of knowledge on peace-related issues.

What is Peacemaking?

By peacemaking we mean to the use of diplomatic means to persuade parties in conflict to cease hostilities and to negotiate a peaceful settlement of their dispute. The United Nations provides various means through which conflicts may be contained and resolved, and their root causes addressed. The Security Council may recommend ways to resolve a dispute or request the Secretary-General's mediation.

The Secretary-General may take diplomatic initiatives to encourage and maintain the momentum of negotiations. The Secretary-General plays a central role in peacemaking, both personally and by dispatching special envoys or missions for specific tasks, such as negotiation or fact-finding. Under the Charter, the Secretary-General may bring to the attention of the Security Council any matter which appears to threaten international peace and security. To help resolve disputes, the Secretary-General may use "good offices for mediating, or to exercise "preventive diplomacy".

It is apt to mention that impartiality of the Secretary-General is one of the United Nations' great assets. In many instances, the Secretary-General has been instrumental in averting a threat to peace or in securing a peace agreement.

Now we should have lookm at peace keeping.

Peacekeeping

In principle, eacekeeping operations, which are authorized by the Security Council, are a crucial instrument at the disposal of the international community to advance international peace and security. The role of peacekeeping was recognized by the world in 1988, when the United Nations peacekeeping forces bagged the Nobel Peace Prize.

It is pertinent to note that though not specifically envisaged in the Charter, peacekeeping was pioneered by the United Nations in 1948 with the establishment of the

United Nations Truce Supervision Organization in the Middle East. Peacekeeping operations are authorized to be deployed by the Security Council with the consent of the host Government, and usually of other parties involved. They may include military and police personnel, together with civilian staff.

Operations may involve military observer missions, peacekeeping forces, or a combination of both. Military observer missions are made up of unarmed officers, typically to monitor an agreement or a ceasefire and the soldiers of the peacekeeping forces have weapons, but in most situations can use them in self-defence only.

It is pertinent to note that military personnel in United Nations peacekeeping operations are voluntarily provided by Member States and are financed by the international community. Participating States are compensated at a standard rate from a special peacekeeping budget.

Preventive Deployment

United Nations action in the former Yugoslav Republic of Macedonia is an example of successful "preventive deployment" — the fielding of peacekeepers to forestall probable conflict.

Concerned about being drawn into the Yugoslav conflict, the country in 1992 requested the deployment of United Nations observers. The Council agreed, and in 1992 dispatched a peacekeeping contingent to the country's borders with Yugoslavia and Albania. Since then, the 1,100-strong *United Nations Preventive Deployment Force* has been monitoring developments in the border areas that could threaten the country's territory or undermine its stability.

The former Yugoslav Republic of Macedonia has repeatedly requested the extension of the mission, which stands as a model for possible future preventive operations.

It is remarkable here that United Nations peacekeeping operations cost some $1.4 billion in 1996 and $1.02 billion in 1997 — less than 0.2 per cent of world military spending. Since 1948, over 750,000 military, police and civilian personnel from some 110 countries have served in these operations; more than 1,500 peacekeepers have lost their lives.

Remarkably, recent years, certain prerequisites for the success of peacekeeping operations have become increasingly clear. These include a genuine desire on the part of combatants to resolve their differences peacefully; a clear mandate; strong political support by the international community; and the provision of the resources necessary to achieve the operation's objectives. At the same time, the unacceptability of inaction has also become obvious. From Yugoslavia to Rwanda, the international community has seen the horrifying destructive effects of contemporary conflicts. In addition, conflicts have major implications beyond the borders of a particular country, and can generate instability through entire regions if they are unchecked.

Even conflicts that are remote from the focus of major Powers can foster problems which have global implications — such as illegal arms flows, terrorism, drug trafficking, refugee flows and environmental degradation. United Nations operations, because of their universality, offer unique advantages as a means to address conflicts. Their universality adds to their legitimacy and limits the implications for the host country's sovereignty.

Peacekeepers from outside a conflict can foster discussion among warring parties while focusing global attention upon local concerns, opening doors that would otherwise remain closed for collective efforts in peacemaking and in building a lasting peace.

Since operations are financed through a United Nations budget and include troops from many countries: this "burden-sharing" can offer extraordinary efficiency in human, financial and political terms.

Operations can take many forms, and are constantly evolving in the light of changing circumstances.

following are the tasks discharged by peacekeeping operations during recent past:

(a) Preventive deployment. Deployed before conflict breaks out, an operation can provide a reassuring presence and a degree of transparency which favour political progress;

(b) Maintenance of ceasefires and separation of forces. By providing "breathing space," an operation based on a limited agreement between parties can foster an atmosphere conducive to negotiations;

(c) Protection of humanitarian operations during conflict. In many conflicts, civilian populations have been deliberately targeted as a means to gain political ends. In such situations, peacekeepers have been asked to provide protection and support for the delivery of humanitarian aid. However, such tasks can place peacekeepers in difficult political positions, and can lead to threats to their own security;

(d) Implementation of a comprehensive settlement. Complex, multidimensional operations, deployed on the basis of comprehensive peace agreements, can assist in such diverse tasks as monitoring human rights, providing electoral assistance, observing elections, furnishing humanitarian assistance and coordinating support for economic reconstruction.

It must be remembered that no list of such roles can be exhaustive. Future conflicts are likely to continue to present complex challenges to the international community. An effective response will require courageous and imaginative use of the tools for peace. Rational and unbiased efforts can only ameliorate the problem.

Role of Regional Organizations

As already mentioned, in the search for peace, the United Nations is increasingly cooperating with regional organizations and other external actors and mechanisms provided for the Charter. It has worked closely with the Organization of American States in Haiti, the Economic Community of West African States in Liberia, the Organization of African Unity (OAU) in Somalia and Western Sahara, and the European Community in the former Yugoslavia. In 1997, the United Nations and the OAU appointed for the first time a joint special representative to address the crises in the Great Lakes region — which includes Burundi, Rwanda and the Democratic Republic of the Congo.

Guiding Peacekeeping Operations

Peacekeeping operations are established by the Security Council and directed by the Secretary-General, often through a special representative; depending on the mission, the Force Commander or the Chief Military Observer is responsible for the military aspects.

In fact, the United Nations has no military force of its own, and Member States provide, on a voluntary basis, the personnel, equipment and logistics required for an operation. Peacekeepers wear their country's uniform: they are identified as peacekeepers only by a United Nations blue helmet or beret and a badge. Military and civilian police personnel serve under the operational control of the United Nations, but remain members of their own national forces. They are expected to conduct themselves in accordance with the exclusively international character of their mission.

Similarly, in Liberia, Georgia and Tajikistan, United Nations military observers have been cooperating with peacekeeping forces of regional organizations. The observers in Tajikistan also cooperate with a civilian mission of the Organization for Security and Cooperation in Europe (OSCE).

In the former Yugoslavia, the United Nations has cooperated with OSCE and the Council of Europe in the areas of human rights, electoral assistance, peacemaking and economic development.

Towards Future Peacekeeping

The international community has drawn lessons from recent peacekeeping experience, and is working to strengthen the United Nations capacity in a number of areas. These include:

- *Enhancing capacity for rapid deployment.* After an operation has been created, its credibility and effectiveness are affected by the promptness with which it is deployed. Rapid deployment can prevent enormous suffering and can spare a country from a legacy of bitterness that can make political reconciliation impossible for years.

  Several initiatives have been taken to address this need:

The United Nations *Standby Arrangements System* provides a framework to facilitate the timely planning and deployment of an operation. As of mid-1998, some 70 Member States had identified troops and equipment that were potentially available for service in operations, subject to approval by national authorities on a case-by-case basis.

Within this system, certain groups of Member States are pursuing initiatives to enhance readiness by pooling their efforts to prepare peacekeepers. One particularly advanced example is the Standby Forces High-Readiness Brigade, whose core staff would be based in Denmark. Troops would remain based in their parent countries and assemble for deployment as necessary. Their capacity for deployment would be enhanced by common procedures and standards for equipment.

In addition, the United Nations is working to create a rapidly deployable mission headquarters, which would constitute a core to be dispatched quickly to the field, around which a peacekeeping operation could be organized.

- *Enhancing ability to function in adversity.* Once deployed, many operations face a difficult or hostile environment. In some situations, an impressive show of force is the best way to avoid having to actually use it. This lesson was successfully applied by the United Nations Transitional Administration in Eastern Slavonia.

  To enhance the influence of the peacekeepers with warring parties, it may be necessary to strengthen not only an operation's capacity to dissuade, but its capacity to persuade. This can be achieved through civic action programmes in which peacekeepers perform helpful tasks to gain people's goodwill and cooperation, or by reinforcing an operation's ability to provide benefits to those who cooperate and make political advances possible.

- *Acting comprehensively.* In assisting States in the aftermath of conflict, peacekeepers often confront problems of economic collapse, traditions of abusive use of the instruments of State to advance political power, and adherence to a system where the winner takes all. If restoring peace is to have any durability or meaning, it must pave the way to a comprehensive response to such problems. The institution-building role of peacekeeping operations has thus increased in importance, with mandates including such tasks as ensuring human rights observance, promoting the means to end impunity of human rights violators, and creating the institutions through which legitimate political differences can be expressed.

One response that offers considerable potential is the deployment of operations that are, built around a core of civilian police, rather than military peacekeepers. These operations can help reshape the dynamics of society after a conflict while strengthening the foundations for lasting peace. The United Nations has also responded by enhancing coordination within operations.

- *Mustering political will.* Ultimately, the success of peacekeeping operations depends on the political will of the warring parties to resolve their differences. It also depends on the political will of Member States to support such operations and ensure that they are provided with the human, material and financial resources necessary for carrying out their mandates. On this basis, peacekeeping can be an effective instrument for managing and resolving conflicts.

Enforcement Measures

The United Nations Charter, the Security Council can take enforcement measures to maintain or restore international peace and security. Such measures range from economic sanctions to international military action.

The Council has resorted to economic sanctions and embargoes as an enforcement tool when peace was threatened and diplomatic efforts had failed. Sanctions were imposed, for instance, against South Africa's apartheid regime in 1977, and subsequently lifted with the end of apartheid in 1994. Recently, sanctions have been imposed against Iraq, the former Yugoslavia, Libya, Haiti, Liberia, Rwanda, Somalia, UNITA forces in Angola, Sudan and Sierra Leone. Economic sanctions have taken many forms, ranging from specific trade bans to full embargoes.

The use of mandatory sanctions brings pressure on a target State or entity to comply with the objectives set by the Security Council without resorting to force. The universal character of the United Nations makes it an especially appropriate body to consider and monitor such measures.

At the same time, Member States have considered the problem of possible unintended consequences of sanctions at various United Nations fora — including the sub-group on sanctions of the General Assembly's Working Group on An Agenda for Peace, where countries have expressed humanitarian concerns on the possible adverse impact of sanctions on the most vulnerable segments of the population, and economic concerns on collateral effects of sanctions.

Authorizing Military Action

When peacemaking efforts fail, stronger action by Member States may be authorized under the Charter. The Council has authorized coalitions of Member States to use "all necessary means", including military action, to deal with a conflict — as it did to restore the sovereignty of Kuwait after its invasion by Iraq (1991); to permit humanitarian relief operations in the midst of civil war in Somalia (1992) and Rwanda (1994); to restore the democratically elected Government in Haiti (1994); and to protect humanitarian operations in Albania (1997).

These actions, though sanctioned by the Security Council, were entirely under the control of the participating States. They were not United Nations peacekeeping operations, which are established by the Security Council and directed by the Secretary-General.

Peace-Building

Today, peace and security are measured not only in terms of the absence of conflict. Lasting peace requires economic development, social justice, environmental protection, democratization, disarmament and respect for human rights. Peace can be durable only if economic and social development are guaranteed.

In the aftermath of a conflict, the United Nations system is thus often called upon to carry out peace-building — action to support structures that will strengthen and consolidate peace. Areas of activity include military security, civil law and order, human rights, elections, local administration, health, education and reconstruction.

Election Monitoring

The United Nations broke new ground in 1989, when it supervised the entire election process which led to the independence of Namibia. Since then, the United Nations has monitored, at Government request, elections in Nicaragua (1990), Haiti (1990), Angola (1992), Cambodia (1993), El Salvador (1994), South Africa (1994), Mozambique (1994), Eastern Slavonia (Croatia, 1997) and Liberia (1997), as well as the referendum on independence in Eritrea (1993).

The degree of United Nations involvement depends upon factors such as the requests received from Governments, peace agreements between previously warring parties, or mandates from the Security Council. The United Nations has played a variety of roles ranging from technical assistance to the actual conduct of the electoral process.

United Nations observers typically follow the electoral campaign, the registration of voters and the organization of the polls. On election day, they are deployed to polling stations throughout the country, observe voting and vote counting, and issue a final statement on the validity of the elections.

Since 1992, the United Nations *Electoral Assistance Division* in the *Department of Political Affairs,* working closely with the United Nations Development Programme (UNDP), which coordinates United Nations electoral assistance in the field, and other offices and programmes, has provided technical assistance in the preparation and holding of elections to over 70 countries. Assistance may involve coordination and support, advisory services, logistics, training, computer applications and short-term observation.

A central tool of United Nations action to consolidate peace is development assistance. Many United Nations organizations — including UNDP, the United Nations Children's Fund (UNICEF), the World Food Programme and the Office of the United Nations High Commissioner for Refugees (UNHCR) — play roles in the recovery stage, which is crucial for providing opportunities for displaced persons and restoring confidence in national and local institutions.

Obviously, the information contained in preceding paragraphs may have made you fully understood the issues of international peace and security in new world order. In the next chapter we will introduce you to some regional security arrangements.

5

Regional Security Arrangements

> "Honest differences of view and honest debate are not disunity. They are the vital process of policy-making among free men."
>
> —*Herbert Hoover*

In fact, the concept of "collective security" forwarded by scholars such as Michael Joseph Savage, Martin Wight, Immanuel Kant, and Woodrow Wilson, are deemed to apply interests in security in a broad manner, to "avoid grouping powers into opposing camps, and refusing to draw dividing lines that would leave anyone out." Tenets of collective security continue to be behind many famous current and historical military alliances, most notably NATO. The term "collective security" has also been cited as a principle of the United Nations, and the League of Nations before that. By employing a system of collective security, the UN hopes to dissuade any member state from acting in a manner likely to threaten peace, thereby avoiding any conflict.

Collective defence (also collective defence) is an arrangement, usually formalized by a treaty and an organization, among participant states that commit support in defence of a member state if it is attacked by another state outside the organization. NATO is the best known collective defence organization. Its now famous Article V calls on (but does not fully commit) member states to assist another member under attack. This article was invoked after the September 11 attacks on the United States, after which other NATO members provided assistance to the US War on Terror in Afghanistan.

Collective defence has its roots in multiparty alliances, and entails benefits as well as risks. On the one hand, by combining and pooling resources, it can reduce any single state's cost of providing fully for its security. Smaller members of NATO, for example, have leeway to invest a greater proportion of their budget on non-military priorities, such as education or health, since they can count on other members to come to their defence, if needed.

On the other hand, collective defence also involves risky commitments. Member states can become embroiled in costly wars in which neither the direct victim nor the aggressor benefit. In the First World War, countries in the collective defence arrangement known as the Triple Entente (France, Britain, Russia) were pulled into war quickly when Russia started full mobilization against Austria-Hungary, whose ally Germany subsequently declared war on Russia.

For collective security and collective defense many organization were formed in different regions of the world. Here in this chapter we will put right on some such organizations.

I. REGIONAL SECURITY SYSTEM

The Regional Security System (RSS) is an international agreement for the defence and security of the eastern Caribbean region. The Regional Security System was created out of a need for collective response to security threats, which were impacting on the stability of the region in the late 1970s and early 1980s. In October 1982 four members of the Organisation of Eastern Caribbean States—namely,

Antigua and Barbuda, Dominica, St. Lucia, and St. Vincent and the Grenadines—signed a memorandum of understanding (MOU) with Barbados to provide for "mutual assistance on request". Saint Kitts and Nevis joined following independence in 1983, and Grenada followed two years later, after Operation Urgent Fury, a combined U.S. and RSS invasion of the country. The MOU was updated in 1992 and the system acquired juridical status in March 1996 under the Treaty which was signed at St. Georges, Grenada.

The RSS initially started as a U.S. instrument to combat the spread of Communism in the Caribbean region. As of 2001, the RSS further cooperates with the CARICOM Regional Task Force on Crime and Security (CRTFCS).

In June 2010, the United States of America and Caribbean regional officials resumed a plan for close cooperation established under the former Partnership for Prosperity and Security in the Caribbean (PPS) from the Clinton era. As part of the joint agreement the United States pledged assistance with the creation of an Eastern Caribbean Coast Guard unit among RSS countries. The Coast Guard unit will underpin the wider US-Caribbean Basin Security Initiative (CBSI) which has deemed the RSS as "central to the CBSI's success, given its reach across the Eastern Caribbean."

Subsequently, the nation of Canada also pledged collaboration with the RSS bloc. to combat a threat of Central American criminal gangs from expanding into the English-speaking Caribbean region. The current member nations are:

- Antigua and Barbuda (since 1982)
- Barbados (since 1982)
- Dominica (since 1982)

- Grenada (since 1985)
- Saint Kitts and Nevis (since 1983)
- Saint Lucia (since 1982)
- Saint Vincent and the Grenadines (since 1982)

Previous Activities

Date	*RSS Operation name*	*Country*	*Reason*
1983	Grenada	Grenada Intervention	Restore a govern-ment in Grenada
1989	Hugo	Antigua, Montserrat and Saint Kitts and Nevis	Assistance in aftermath of Hurricane Hugo
1990	Coup	Trinidad and Tobago	Aftermath of an attempted Coup d'état in Trinidad and Tobago
1994	Internal Security	Saint Kitts and Nevis	Prison riot
1995	Luis, Marilyn	Antigua and Saint Kitts and Nevis	Assistance in aftermath of Hurricane Luis and Hurricane Marilyn
1998	Georges	Saint Kitts and Nevis	Assistance in aftermath of Hurricane Georges
1998	Weedeater	Saint Vincent and the Grenadines	Eradication of Cannabis
2003	Bordelais	Saint Lucia	Transfer prisoners to new prison facility
2004	Ivan Relief Efforts	Grenada	Assistance in aftermath of Hurricane Ivan
2006	Glendairy	Barbados	Prison uprising
2010	Haiti	Haiti	Assistance in aftermath of the Haiti 2010 Earthquake

The R.S.S., as it is commonly referred to, is based in Barbados at the Paragon Centre, headed by many regional army chiefs. It mainly serves as a defence system for the Caribbean Sea, conducting many operations by detecting and combating cross-Atlantic and intra-Caribbean drug smuggling, protection of the sovereignty of the nations of the Caribbean, providing assistance to Caribbean countries at the request of governments and are usually the first to respond after natural disasters occur, such as hurricanes, floods and earthquakes.

II. ORGANISATION OF EASTERN CARIBBEAN STATES (OECS)

The Organisation of Eastern Caribbean States (OECS), created in 1981, is an inter-governmental organisation dedicated to economic harmonisation and integration, protection of human and legal rights, and the encouragement of good governance between countries and dependencies in the Eastern Caribbean. It also performs the role of spreading responsibility and liability in the event of natural disaster, such as a hurricane.

The main organ of the OECS, the Secretariat, is based in the capital city of Castries, Saint Lucia.

Coming to history, the OECS was created on 18 June 1981, with the Treaty of Basseterre, which was named after the city of the same name, the capital city of St. Kitts and Nevis. The OECS is the successor of the Leewards Islands' political organisation known as the West Indies Associated States (WISA). One prominent aspect of the modern day OECS economic bloc has been the accelerated pace of trans-national integration among its member states.

It is apt to mention here that all of the members-states of the OECS are either Full or Associate members of the Caribbean Community and were among the second batch of countries that joined the CARICOM Single Market and Economy (CSME).

Membership

The OECS currently has nine members, spread across the Eastern Caribbean. Together, they form a near-continuous archipelago across the Leeward Islands and Windward Islands.

The two most geographically isolated members, Anguilla and the British Virgin Islands, have only associate membership of the organisation. As a result, diplomatic missions of the OECS do not represent these two states. For the purposes of further discussing the membership, they are treated as equals of the full members.

Six of the members were formerly colonies of the United Kingdom. The other three, Anguilla, the British Virgin Islands, and Montserrat remain overseas territories of the UK. Eight of the nine members consider Queen Elizabeth II to be sovereign (Dominica is a republic). There is no requirement for the members to have been British colonies, however the close historical, cultural and economic relationship fostered by them having all been British colonies is as much a factor in the membership of the OECS as their geographical proximity. As well, the Queen's likeness appears on the East Caribbean dollar's coins and banknotes.

All seven full members are also the founding members of the OECS, having been a part of the organisation since its founding on 18 June 1981. The British Virgin Islands was the first associate member, joining on 22 November 1984 and Anguilla is the latest associate member, having joined in 1995.

In fact, although all of the current full and associate members are all past or present British dependencies, other islands in the region have expressed interest in becoming associate members of the OECS. The first was the United States Virgin Islands, which applied for associate membership in February 1990 and requested that US Federal Government allow the territory to participate as such. At that time, it was felt by the US government that it was not an appropriate time to make such a request.

Membership status	*Description*
Membership	Antigua and Barbuda
	Dominica
	Grenada
	Montserrat
	Saint Kitts and Nevis
	Saint Lucia
	Saint Vincent and the Grenadines
Associate membership	Anguilla
	British Virgin Islands

However, the US Virgin Islands remained interested in the OECS and, as of 2002, stated that it would revisit the issue with the US government at a later date. In 2001, Saba, an island of the Netherlands Antilles, decided to seek membership in the OECS. Saba's Island Council had passed a motion on May 30, 2001 calling for Saba's membership in the organisation and subsequently on June 7, 2001, the Executive Council of Saba decided in favour of membership. Saba's senator in the Netherlands Antilles parliament was then asked to present a motion requesting the Antillean parliament to support Saba's quest for membership.

Besides the support from the Antillean parliament, Saba also required a dispensation from the government of the Kingdom of the Netherlands to become an associate member of the OECS. Saba's bid for membership was reportedly supported by St. Kitts and Nevis and discussed at the 34th meeting of OECS leaders in Dominica in July. Also in 2001, Sint Maarten, another part of the Netherlands Antilles, explored the possibility of joining the OECS. After learning of Saba's intentions to join, St. Maarten suggested exploring ways in which Saba and St. Maarten could support each other in their pursuit of membership.

It must be remembered that none of the prospective members have become associate members as yet, but Saba, St. Eustatius and St. Maarten do participate in the meetings of the Council of Tourism Ministers (as the Forum of Tourism Ministers of the Eastern Caribbean, along with representatives of Saint-Martin, Saint Barthélemy, Martinique and Guadeloupe).

Recent Developments

Remarkably, on 13 August 2008 the leaders of Trinidad and Tobago, Grenada, St. Lucia, and St. Vincent and the Grenadines announced their intention to pursue a sub-regional political union within CARICOM. As part of the preliminary discussions the Heads of Government for the involved states announced that 2011 would see their states entering into an economic union. Following that date, 2013 is supposed to be the date of full political union for the members involved.

Further, it is remarkable that in 2008 the heads of the OECS also received a request from Venezuela to join the grouping.

The OECS Director General Len Ishmael confirmed Venezuela's application was discussed at the 48th Meeting of the OECS Authority held in Montserrat. But she said OECS decision makers within the sub-region were yet to determine whether membership should be granted for Venezuela.

Administrative Structure

Secretariat: The functions of the Organisation are set out in the Treaty of Basseterre and are coordinated by the Secretariat under the direction and management of the Director General.

The OECS functions in a rapidly changing international economic environment, characterised by globalisation and trade liberalisation which are posing serious challenges to the economic and social stability of their small island members.

It is the purpose of the Organisation to assist its Members to respond to these multi-faceted challenges by identifying scope for joint or coordinated action towards the economic and social advancement of their countries. The restructuring of the Secretariat was informed by considerations of cost effectiveness in the context of the need to respond to the increasing challenges placed on it, taking into account the limited fiscal capacities of its members. The Secretariat consists of four main Divisions responsible for: External Relations, Functional Cooperation, Corporate Services and Economic Affairs.

These four Divisions oversee the work of a number of specialised institutions, work units or projects located in six countries: Antigua/Barbuda, Commonwealth of Dominica, St Lucia, Belgium, Canada, and the United States of America.

Further, in carrying out its mission, the OECS works along with a number of sub-regional and regional agencies and institutions. These include the Eastern Caribbean Central Bank (ECCB); the Caribbean Community (Caricom) Secretariat; the Caribbean Regional Negotiating Machinery (RNM) and the Caribbean Development Bank (CDB).

Director General: The authority within the OECS

Secretariat is led by the Director General. The current Director General of the OECS is Dr. Len Ishmael.

Eastern Caribbean Supreme Court: The Eastern Caribbean Supreme Court (ECSC), which was created during the era of WISA, today handles the judicial matters in the Organisation of Eastern Caribbean States. When a trial surpasses the stage of High Court in an OECS member state, it can then be passed on to the ECSC at the level of Supreme court. Cases appealed from the stage of ECSC Supreme Court will then be referred to the jurisdiction of the Judicial Committee of the Privy Council. The Caribbean Court of Justice (CCJ) was established in 2003, but constitutional changes need to be put in place before the CCJ becomes the final Court of Appeal.

Activities

Passport: A common OECS Passport was originally planned for January 1, 2003 but its introduction was delayed. At the 38th OECS Authority Meeting in January 2004, the Secretariat was mandated to have the two companies expressing an interest in producing the common passport (De La Rue Identity Systems and the Canadian Banknote Company) make presentations at the next (39th) Authority Meeting. At the 39th Meeting the critical issue of the relationship between the OECS passport and the CARICOM passport was discussed and at the 40th OECS Authority Meeting in November 2004, the OECS Heads of Government agreed to give CARICOM a further 6 months (until May 2005) to introduce a CARICOM Passport.

Failure to introduce the CARICOM Passport by that time would have resulted in the OECS moving ahead with its plans to introduce the OECS Passport. As the CARICOM Passport was first introduced in January 2005 (by Suriname) then the idea of the OECS Passport was abandoned. Had the passport been introduced however it would not have been issued to Economic Citizens within the OECS states.

Economic Union: It is pertinent to note that the decision to establish an economic union was taken by OECS Heads of Government at the 34th meeting of the Authority held in Dominica in July 2001. At the 35th meeting of the Authority in Anguilla in January 2002, the main elements of an economic union implementation project were endorsed. The project was expected to be implemented over a two-year period with seven of the nine OECS member states (i.e. Antigua and Barbuda, Dominica, Grenada, Montserrat, St. Kitts and Nevis, St. Lucia and St. Vincent and the Grenadines) participating in the economic union initiative.

The remaining two member states, Anguilla and the British Virgin Islands, would not have participated immediately, but would have requested time to consider the issue further. In 2003, work had been initiated on the central issue of the creation of new Treaty arrangements to replace the Treaty of Basseterre which established the OECS. Among the elements of the project was the creation of a technical committee for a draft OECS Economic Union Treaty. This technical committee was inaugurated on May 4, 2004 and began designing the draft Treaty.

The new OECS Economic Union Treaty was finally presented at the 43rd OECS Meeting in St. Kitts on June 21, 2006. The current draft Treaty was commended at the meeting, but the Authority directed the formulation of some additional provisions to allow a role for national parliamentary representatives (both government and opposition) of the Member States in the form of a regional Assembly of Parliamentarians. This body, it was felt, was necessary to act as a legislative filter to the Authority in its law making capacity.

The Heads further directed that the Treaty be reviewed by a meeting of members of the Task Force, Attorneys General, the draftsperson for the Treaty and representatives of the OECS Secretariat. The presentation of the Treaty at the Meeting was followed by the signing of a Declaration of Intent to implement the Treaty by the Heads of Government or their representatives (except that of the British Virgin Islands).

It was agreed in the Declaration, that implementation of the Treaty would occur only after a year of public consultation, through a mass national and regional education programme with strong political leadership and direction. According to the Declaration, the Treaty is to be signed, and the Economic Union is to be established by July 1, 2007.

In fact, the provisions of the Economic Union Treaty are expected to include:

(a) The free circulation of goods and trade in services within the OECS

(b) Free movement of labour by December 2007

(c) The free movement of capital (via support of the money and capital market programme of the Eastern Caribbean Central Bank)

(d) A regional Assembly of Parliamentarians

(e) A common external tariff.

It is apt to mention that some of these provisions would already have been covered to some extent by the CSME, but some, such as the Assembly of Parliamentarians, would be unique to the OECS. Although some of the provisions would seem to duplicate efforts by the CSME, the Declaration of Intent and statements by some OECS leaders, acknowledge the CSME and give assurance that the OECS Economic Union would not run counter to CARICOM integration but that it would become seamlessly integrated into the CSME.

To this end, the OECS Heads of Government agreed that steps should be taken to ensure that the OECS Economic Union Treaty would be recognised under the Revised Treaty of Chaguaramas, just as the original Treaty of Chaguaramas had recognised the Treaty of Basseterre.

Central Bank: The majority of the OECS members-states are participants of the Eastern Caribbean Central Bank (ECCB) monetary authority. The regional central bank oversees financial and banking integrity for the Organisation of Eastern Caribbean States economic bloc of states. Part of the bank's oversight lends to maintaining the financial integrity of the Eastern Caribbean dollar (XCD). Of all OECS member-states, only the British Virgin Islands do not use the Eastern Caribbean dollar as their de facto native currency.

On Security

It is remarkable here that the OECS sub-region has a military support unit known as the Regional Security System (RSS). It is made up of the independent countries of the OECS along with Barbados. The unit is based in the island of Barbados and receives funding and training from various countries including the United States, Canada and the People's Republic of China.

III. ARAB LEAGUE

The Arab League, officially called the League of Arab States, is a regional organization of Arab states in Southwest Asia, and North and Northeast Africa. It was formed in Cairo on March 22, 1945 with six members: Egypt, Iraq, Transjordan (renamed Jordan after 1946), Lebanon, Saudi

Arabia, and Syria. Yemen joined as a member on May 5, 1945.

The Arab League currently has 22 members and four observers. The main goal of the league is to "draw closer the relations between member States and co-ordinate collaboration between them, to safeguard their independence and sovereignty, and to consider in a general way the affairs and interests of the Arab countries." Through institutions such as the Arab League Educational, Cultural and Scientific Organization (ALESCO) and the Economic and Social Council of the Arab League's Council of Arab Economic Unity (CAEU), the Arab League facilitates political, economic, cultural, scientific and social programs designed to promote the interests of the Arab world. It has served as a forum for the member states to coordinate their policy positions, to deliberate on matters of common concern, to settle some Arab disputes, and to limit conflicts such as the 1958 Lebanon crisis.

The League has served as a platform for the drafting and conclusion of many landmark documents promoting economic integration. One example is the *Joint Arab Economic Action Charter* which sets out the principles for economic activities in the region. Each member state has one vote in the League Council, while decisions are binding only for those states that have voted for them. The aims of the league in 1945 were to strengthen and coordinate the political, cultural, economic, and social programs of its members, and to mediate disputes among them or between them and third parties. Furthermore, the signing of an agreement on *Joint Defence and Economic Cooperation* on April 13, 1950 committed the signatories to coordination of military defence measures.

The Arab league has played an important role in shaping school curricula, advancing the role of women in the Arab societies, promoting child welfare, encouraging youth and sports programs, preserving Arab cultural heritage, and fostering cultural exchanges between the member states. Literacy campaigns have been launched, intellectual works reproduced, and modern technical terminology is translated for the use within member states. The league encourages measures against crime and drug abuse, and deals with labour issues—particularly among the emigrant Arab workforce.

Members

The Arab League was founded in Cairo in 1945 by Egypt, Iraq, Lebanon, Saudi Arabia, Syria, Transjordan (Jordan from 1946), and Yemen. There was a continual increase in membership during the second half of the 20th century, with additional 15 Arab states and 4 observers being admitted. Egypt's membership was suspended in 1979 after it signed the Egyptian–Israeli Peace Treaty, and the League's headquarters were moved from Cairo to Tunis. In 1987, Arab countries restored diplomatic relations with Egypt and the country was readmitted to the league in 1989 while the league's headquarters moved back to Cairo. In September 2006, Venezuela was accepted as an observer, and India in 2007.

Israel is not a member despite 20% of its population being of Arab origin, nearly half the Jewish population being descended from Jews from Arab countries, and Arabic being an official language. Neither is Chad a member, although Arabic is in both official and vernacular use there.

Four countries are observer states — a status that entitles them to express their opinion and give advice but denies them voting rights.

The area of members of the Arab League covers around

14 million km^2 and straddles two continents: Western Asia as well as Northern and Northeastern Africa. The area consists of large arid deserts, namely the Sahara. Nevertheless, it also contains several very fertile lands, such as the Nile Valley, the High Atlas Mountains, and the Fertile Crescent which stretches from Iraq over Syria and Lebanon to Palestine. The area comprises also deep forests in southern Arabia and southern Sudan as well as the major parts of the world's longest river—the Nile.

The area has witnessed the rise and fall of many ancient civilizations: Ancient Egypt, Rome, Ancient Israel, Assyria, Babylon, Phoenicia, Carthage, Kush, and Nabateans.

Governance

The Charter of the Arab League endorsed the principle of an Arab homeland while respecting the sovereignty of the individual member states. The internal regulations of the Council of the League and the committees were agreed in October 1951. Those of the Secretariat-General were agreed in May 1953.

Since then, governance of the Arab League has been based on the duality of supra-national institutions and the sovereignty of the member states. Preservation of individual statehood derived its strengths from the natural preference of ruling elites to maintain their power and independence in decision making. Moreover, the fear of the richer that the poorer may share their wealth in the name of Arab nationalism, the feuds among Arab rulers, and the influence of external powers that might oppose Arab unity can be seen as obstacles towards a deeper integration of the league.

Economy

It is pertinent to note that Arab League is rich in resources, with enormous oil and natural gas resources; it also has great fertile lands in South of the Sudan, usually referred to as the food basket of the Arab World. The region's instability has not affected its tourism industry, that is considered the fastest growing industry in the region, with Egypt, UAE, Algeria, Tunisia, and Jordan leading the way. Another industry that is growing steadily in the Arab League is telecommunications. Within less than a decade, local companies such as Orascom and Etisalat have managed to compete internationally. Economic achievements initiated by the League amongst member states have been less impressive than those achieved by other smaller Arab organizations such as the Gulf Cooperation Council (GCC). However, several promising major economic projects are set to be completed soon. Among them is the Arab Gas Pipeline, scheduled to be accomplished in 2010. It will transport Egyptian and Iraqi gas to Jordan, Syria, Lebanon, and Turkey.

The Greater Arab Free Trade Area (GAFTA), planned to come into effect on January 1, 2008, will render 95% of all Arab products free of customs. Economic development in the Arab League is very disparate. Significant difference in wealth and economic conditions exist between the rich oil states of UAE, Qatar, Kuwait, and Algeria on the one hand, and poor countries like the Comoros, Mauritania, and Djibouti on the other hand. Arab economic funding is under development. As an example, the Arab League agreed to support the Sudanese region of Darfur with 500 million dollars, and Egyptian and Libyan companies are planning to build several wells in this dry area.

On Status of Palestine

Mindful of their previous announcements in support of the Arabs of Palestine the framers of the Pact were determined to include them within the league from its inauguration. This was done by means of an annex that declared:

> "Even though Palestine was not able to control her own destiny, it was on the basis of the recognition of her independence that the Covenant of the League of Nations determined a system of government for her. Her existence and her independence among the nations can, therefore, no more be questioned *de jure* than the independence of any of the other Arab States. [...] Therefore, the States signatory to the Pact of the Arab League consider that in view of Palestine's special circumstances, the Council of the League should designate an Arab delegate from Palestine to participate in its work until this country enjoys actual independence."

At the Cairo Summit of 1964, the Arab League initiated the creation of an organization representing the Palestinian people. The first Palestinian National Council convened in East Jerusalem on May 29, 1964. The Palestinian Liberation Organization was founded during this meeting on June 2, 1964.

At the Beirut Summit on March 28, 2002 the league adopted the Arab Peace Initiative, a Saudi-inspired peace plan for the Arab-Israeli conflict. The initiative offered full normalization of the relations with Israel. In exchange, Israel was demanded to withdraw from all occupied territories, including the Golan Heights, to recognize an independent Palestinian state in the West Bank and the Gaza Strip with East Jerusalem as its capital, as well as a "just solution" for the Palestinian refugees.

The Peace Initiative was again endorsed at 2007 in the Riyadh Summit. In July 2007, the Arab League sent a mission, consisting of the Jordanian and Egyptian foreign ministers, to Israel to promote the initiative. The mission was welcomed with reservations by Israel. Following Venezuela's move to expel the resident Israeli diplomats amid the 2008–2009 Israel–Gaza conflict, Kuwaiti member of parliament Waleed al-Tabtabai made a public plea to move the Arab League headquarters from Cairo to Caracas, Venezuela.

The Arab League is a culturally and ethnically diverse association of 22 member states, although a vast majority of the league consist of Arab people. As of January 1, 2007, about 314,000,000 people live in the states of the Arab League. Its population grows faster than in most other global regions. This threatens to diminish the slow economic expansion expected in the league's developing countries.

The most populous member state is Egypt, with a population of about 80 million. The least populated is Djibouti, with about 500,000 inhabitants. Most of the Persian Gulf Arab states have large populations of foreign labourers. The UAE's Arab population counts for less than 20% of its total population, while 50% originate from South-and Southeast Asia, although they are not citizens. Some Persian Gulf Arab states also import cheap Arab labour, mainly from Egypt, Yemen, and Somalia.

Since large parts of the Arab League are deserts, the population is concentrated in and around cities where most the trade and industry are located. The largest Arab cities are Cairo, followed by Baghdad, Khartoum, Giza, Damascus, Riyadh, and Casablanca.

IV. CIS (COMMONWEALTH OF INDEPENDENT STATES)

The Commonwealth of Independent States (CIS) is a regional organization whose participating countries are former Soviet Republics, formed during the breakup of the Soviet Union.

The CIS is comparable to a very loose association of states and in no way comparable to a federation, confederation or supra-national organisation such as the old European Community. It is more comparable to the Commonwealth of Nations. Although the CIS has few supranational powers, it is more than a purely symbolic organization, possessing coordinating powers in the realm of trade, finance, lawmaking, and security. It has also promoted cooperation on democratization and cross-border crime prevention. As a regional organization, CIS participates in UN peacekeeping forces. Some of the members of the CIS have established the Eurasian Economic Community with the aim of creating a full-fledged common market.

The CIS organization was founded on 8 December 1991 by the Republic of Belarus, the Russian Federation, and Ukraine, when the leaders of the three countries met in the Belovezhskaya Pushcha Natural Reserve, about 50 km (30 miles) north of Brest in Belarus and signed a *Creation Agreement* on the dissolution of the Soviet Union and the creation of CIS as a successor entity to the USSR. At the same time they announced that the new alliance would be open to all republics of the former Soviet Union, as well as other nations sharing the same goals. The CIS charter stated that all the members were sovereign and independent nations and thereby effectively abolished the Soviet Union.

On 21 December 1991, the leaders of eight additional former Soviet Republics – Armenia, Azerbaijan, Kazakhstan, Kyrgyzstan, Moldova, Turkmenistan, Tajikistan, and Uzbekistan – agreed to join the CIS, thus bringing the number of participating countries to 11. Georgia joined two years later, in December 1993. As of that time, 12 of the 15 former Soviet Republics participated in the CIS. Three former Soviet Republics, the Baltic states of Estonia, Latvia, and Lithuania chose not to join.

In March 2007, Igor Ivanov, the secretary of the Russian Security Council, expressed his doubts concerning the usefulness of CIS, and emphasizing that the Eurasian Economic Community became a more competent organization to unify the biggest countries of the CIS. In May 2009 the six countries Armenia, Azerbaijan, Belarus, Georgia, Moldova and Ukraine joined the Eastern

Partnership, a project which was initiated by the European Union (EU).

Military Structures

When Yeltsin became Russian Defence Minister on 7 May 1992, Yevgeny Shaposhnikov, the man appointed as Commander-in-Chief of the CIS Armed Forces, and his staff, were ejected from the MOD and General Staff buildings and given offices in the former Warsaw Pact Headquarters at 41 Leningradsky Prospekt on the northern outskirts of Moscow. Shaposhnikov resigned in June 1993.

In December 1993, the CIS Armed Forces Headquarters was abolished. Instead, 'the CIS Council of Defence Ministers created a CIS Military Cooperation Coordination Headquarters (MCCH) in Moscow, with 50 per cent of the funding provided by Russia.' General Victor Samsonov was appointed as Chief of Staff.

Membership

The Creation Agreement remained the main constituent document of the CIS until January 1993, when the *CIS Charter* was adopted. The charter formalized the concept of membership: a member country is defined as a country that ratifies the CIS Charter (sec. 2, art. 7). Turkmenistan has not ratified the charter and changed its CIS standing to associate member as of 26 August 2005 in order to be consistent with its UN-recognized international neutrality status. Although Ukraine was one of the three founding countries and ratified the Creation Agreement in December 1991, Ukraine did not to ratify the CIS Charter and is not a member of the CIS

V. EUROPEAN UNION

The European Union (EU) is an economic and political union of 27 member states, located primarily in Europe. Committed to regional integration, the EU was established by the Treaty of Maastricht on 1 November 1993 upon the foundations of the European Economic Community. With almost 500 million citizens, the EU combined generates an estimated 30% share (US$18.4 trillion in 2008) of the nominal gross world product and about 22% of the PPP gross world product.

The EU has developed a single market through a standardised system of laws which apply in all member states, ensuring the free movement of people, goods, services, and capital. It maintains common policies on trade, agriculture, fisheries and regional development. Sixteen member states have adopted a common currency, the euro, constituting the Eurozone. The EU has developed a limited role in foreign policy, having representation at the WTO, G8, G20 and at the UN. It enacts legislation in justice and home affairs, including the abolition of passport controls by the Schengen agreement between 22 EU and 3 non-EU states.

As an international organisation, the EU operates through a hybrid system of supranationalism and intergovernmentalism. In certain areas, decisions are made through negotiation between member states, while in others, independent supranational institutions are responsible without a requirement for unanimity between member states. Important institutions and bodies of the EU include the European Commission, the Council of the European Union, the European Council, the European Court of Justice, and the European Central Bank. The European Parliament is elected every five years by member states' citizens, to whom the citizenship of the European Union is guaranteed.

The EU originates from the European Coal and Steel Community formed among six countries in 1951 and the Treaty of Rome in 1957. Since then, the EU has evolved through a process of enlargement, while new policy areas have been added to the remit of its institutions. After the end of the World War II, moves towards European integration were seen by many as an escape from the extreme forms of nationalism which had devastated the continent. One such attempt to unite Europeans was the European Coal and Steel Community which, while having the modest aim of centralised control of the previously national coal and steel industries of its member states, was declared to be "a first step in the federation of Europe". The originators and supporters of the Community include Jean Monnet, Robert Schuman, Paul Henri Spaak and Alcide de Gasperi. The founding members of the Community were Belgium, France, Italy, Luxembourg, the Netherlands and West Germany.

In fact, in 1957, these six countries signed the Treaties of Rome which extended the earlier cooperation within the European Coal and Steel Community and created the European Economic Community, (EEC) establishing a customs union and the European Atomic Energy Community (Euratom) for cooperation in developing nuclear energy. In 1967 the Merger Treaty created a single set of institutions for the three communities, which were collectively referred to as the *European Communities* (EC), although commonly just as the *European Community*.

In 1973 the Communities enlarged to include Denmark, Ireland and the United Kingdom. Norway had negotiated to join at the same time but Norwegian voters rejected membership in a referendum and so Norway remained outside. In 1979 the first direct, democratic elections to the European Parliament were held.

Greece joined in 1981, and Spain and Portugal in 1986. In 1985 the Schengen Agreement led the way toward the creation of open borders without passport controls between most member states and some non-member states. In 1986 the European flag began to be used by the Community and the Single European Act was signed.

In 1990, after the fall of the Iron Curtain, the former East Germany became part of the Community as part of a newly united Germany. With enlargement toward Eastern and Central Europe on the agenda, the Copenhagen criteria for candidate members to join the European Union were agreed.

The European Union was formally established when the Maastricht Treaty came into force on 1 November 1993, and in 1995 Austria, Sweden and Finland joined the newly established EU. In 2002, euro notes and coins replaced national currencies in 12 of the member states. Since then, the eurozone has increased to encompass sixteen countries, with Slovakia joining the eurozone on 1 January 2009. In 2004, the EU saw its biggest enlargement to date when Malta, Cyprus, Slovenia, Estonia, Latvia, Lithuania, Poland, the Czech Republic, Slovakia, and Hungary joined the Union.

On 1 January 2007, Romania and Bulgaria became the EU's newest members and Slovenia adopted the euro. In June 2009 the 2009 elections which later led to a renewal of Barroso's Commission Presidency and in July of that year iceland formally applied for EU membership. On 1 December 2009 the Lisbon Treaty came into force after a protracted and controversial birth. This reformed many aspects of the EU but in particular created a permanent President of the European Council, the first of which is Herman van Rompuy, and a strengthened High Representative; Catherine Ashton.

Member States

Only six of these – France, (then-West) Germany, Italy, and the three already integrated Benelux countries; Belgium, Netherlands, and Luxembourg – were members at the start, with membership having grown as countries willingly accede to the treaties and by doing so, pool sovereignty in exchange for representation in the institutions. To join the EU a country must meet the Copenhagen criteria, defined at the 1993 Copenhagen European Council. These require a stable democracy that respects human rights and the rule of law; a functioning market economy capable of competition within the EU; and the acceptance of the obligations of membership, including EU law. Evaluation of a country's fulfilment of the criteria is the responsibility of the European Council.

No member state has ever left the Union, although Greenland (an autonomous province of Denmark) withdrew in 1985. The Lisbon Treaty now provides a clause dealing with how a member leaves the EU.

There are three official candidate countries, Croatia, Macedonia and Turkey. Albania, Bosnia and Herzegovina, Montenegro, Serbia and Iceland are officially recognised as potential candidates. Kosovo is also listed as a potential candidate but the European Commission does not list it as an independent country because not all member states recognise it as an independent country separate from Serbia.

Four Western European countries that have chosen not to join the EU have partly committed to the EU's economy and regulations: Iceland, which has now applied for membership, Liechtenstein and Norway, which are a part of the single market through the European Economic Area, and Switzerland, which has similar ties through bilateral treaties. The relationships of the European microstates, Andorra, Monaco, San Marino and the Vatican include the use of the euro and other areas of co-operation.

Governance

The EU's work is divided into three areas of responsibility, called *pillars*. The original European Community policies form the first pillar, while the second consists of Common Foreign and Security Policy. The third pillar originally consisted of Justice and Home Affairs, however owing to changes introduced by the Amsterdam and Nice treaties, it has been reduced to Police and Judicial Co-operation in Criminal Matters (other matters were transferred to the Community). Broadly speaking, the second and third pillars can be described as the intergovernmental pillars because the supranational institutions of the Commission, Parliament and the Court of Justice play less of a role or none at all, while the lead is taken by the intergovernmental Council of Ministers and the European Council (which operate more by consensus than majority in these pillars). Most activities of the EU come under the first, Community pillar.

This is mostly an economically oriented pillar and is where the supranational institutions have the most influence. Herman Van Rompuy was chosen on 19 November 2009 to become the first permanent President of the European Council, a position he will take up on 1 January 2010. The activities of the EU are regulated by a number of institutions and bodies. They carry out the tasks and policies set out for them in the treaties. The EU receives its political leadership from the European Council, which is composed of one representative per member state—either its head of state or head of government—plus the President of the Commission.

Each member state's representative is assisted by its Foreign Minister. The European Council uses its leadership role to sort out disputes which have arisen between member states and the institutions, and to resolve political crises and disagreements over controversial issues and policies. These procedures are all subject to the principle of subsidiarity which requires that action only be taken at EU level where an objective cannot be sufficiently achieved by the member states alone.

By virtue of a rotating presidency, every member state

takes the helm of the EU for a period of six months during which that country's representatives chair meetings of the European Council and the Council of Ministers. The member state holding the presidency typically uses it to drive a particular policy agenda such as economic reform, reform of the EU itself, enlargement or furthering European integration. The European Council usually meet four times a year at European Summits.

Institutions

The European Commission acts as the EU's executive arm and is responsible for initiating legislation and the day-to-day running of the EU. It is intended to act solely in the interest of the EU as a whole, as opposed to the Council which consists of leaders of member states who reflect national interests. The commission is also seen as the motor of European integration. It is currently composed of 27 commissioners for different areas of policy, one from each member state. The President of the Commission and all the other commissioners are nominated by the Council. Appointment of the Commission President, and also the Commission in its entirety, have to be confirmed by Parliament.

The European Parliament forms one half of the EU's legislature. The 736 Members of the European Parliament (MEPs) are directly elected by EU citizens every five years. Although MEPs are elected on a national basis, they sit according to political groups rather than their nationality. Each country has a set number of seats. The Parliament and the Council of Ministers form and pass legislation jointly, using co-decision, in certain areas of policy. This procedure has extend to many new areas under the Treaty of Lisbon, and hence increase the power and relevance of the Parliament. The Parliament also has the power to reject or censure the Commission and the EU budget. The President of the European Parliament carries out the role of speaker in parliament and represents it externally. The president and vice presidents are elected by MEPs every two and a half years.

The Council of the European Union (sometimes referred to as the Council of Ministers) forms the other half of the EU's legislature. It consists of a government minister from each member states and meets in different compositions depending on the policy area being addressed. Notwithstanding its different compositions, it is considered to be one single body. In addition to its legislative functions, the Council also exercises executive functions in relations to the Common Foreign and Security Policy.

The judicial branch of the EU consists of the European Court of Justice (ECJ) and the Court of First Instance. Together they interpret and apply the treaties and the law of the EU. The Court of First Instance mainly deals with cases taken by individuals and companies directly before the EU's courts, and the ECJ primarily deals with cases taken by member states, the institutions and cases referred to it by the courts of member states. Decisions from the Court of First Instance can be appealed to the Court of Justice but only on a point of law.

Foreign Relations

Foreign policy cooperation between member states dates from the establishment of the Community in 1957, when member states negotiated as a bloc in international trade negotiations under the Common Commercial Policy. Steps for a more wide ranging coordination in foreign relations began in 1970 with the establishment of European Political Cooperation which created an informal consultation process between member states with the aim of forming common foreign policies. It was not, however, until 1987 when European Political Cooperation was introduced on a formal basis by the Single European Act. EPC was renamed as the *Common Foreign and Security Policy* (CFSP) by the Maastricht Treaty.

The Maastricht Treaty gives the CFSP the aims of promoting both the EU's own interests and those of the international community as a whole. This includes promoting international co-operation, respect for human rights, democracy, and the rule of law.

The Amsterdam Treaty created the office of the High Representative for the Common Foreign and Security Policy (currently held by Catherine Ashton) to co-ordinate the EU's foreign policy. The High Representative, in conjunction with the current Presidency, speaks on behalf of the EU in foreign policy matters and can have the task of articulating ambiguous policy positions created by disagreements among member states. The Common Foreign and Security Policy requires unanimity among the now 27 member states on the appropriate policy to follow on any particular issue. The unanimity and difficult issues treated under the CFSP makes disagreements, such as those which occurred over the war in Iraq, not uncommon.

Besides the emerging international policy of the European Union, the international influence of the EU is also felt through enlargement. The perceived benefits of becoming a member of the EU act as an incentive for both political and economic reform in states wishing to fulfil the EU's accession criteria, and are considered an important factor contributing to the reform of former Communist countries in Central and Eastern Europe. This influence on the internal affairs of other countries is generally referred to as "soft power", as opposed to military "hard power".

In the UN, as an observer and working together, the EU has gained influence in areas such as aid due to its large contributions in that field. In the G8, the EU has rights of membership besides chairing/hosting summit meetings and is represented at meetings by the presidents of the Commission and the Council. In the World Trade Organisation (WTO), where all 27 member states are represented, the EU as a body is represented by Trade Commissioner Benita Ferrero-Waldner.

There has been discussion among political analysts as to whether the European Union represents a new type of geopolitical actor that focuses on supranational law and economic and political rivalries rather than military and ideological rivalries. The discussion is typified by the debate over the extent to which the European Union sees itself, or is seen by others, as a "postmodern superpower" – either now or in the foreseeable future.

Military and Defence

The predecessors of the European Union were not devised as a strong military alliance because NATO was largely seen as appropriate and sufficient for defence purposes. Twenty-one EU members are members of NATO while the remaining member states follow policies of neutrality. The Western European Union (WEU) is a European security organisation related to the EU. In 1992, the WEU's relationship with the EU was defined, when the EU assigned it the "Petersberg tasks" (humanitarian missions such as peacekeeping and crisis management). These tasks were later transferred from the WEU to the EU by the Amsterdam Treaty and now form part of the Common Foreign and Security Policy and the European Security and Defence Policy. Elements of the WEU are currently being merged into the Common Foreign and Security Policy, and the President of the WEU is currently the EU's foreign policy chief.

Following the Kosovo War in 1999, the European Council agreed that "the Union must have the capacity for autonomous action, backed by credible military forces, the means to decide to use them, and the readiness to do so, in order to respond to international crises without prejudice to actions by NATO". To that end, a number of efforts were made to increase the EU's military capability, notably the Helsinki Headline Goal process. After much discussion, the most concrete result was the EU Battlegroups initiative, each of which is planned to be able to deploy quickly about 1500 men. EU forces have been deployed on peacekeeping missions from Africa to the former Yugoslavia and the Middle East. EU military operations are supported by a number of bodies, including the European Defence Agency, satellite centre and the military staff. In an EU consisting of 27 members, substantial security and defence cooperation is increasingly relying on great power cooperation.

Humanitarian Aid

The European Community Humanitarian Aid Office, or "ECHO", provides humanitarian aid from the EU to developing countries. In 2006 its budget amounted to €671 million, 48% of which went to the African, Caribbean and Pacific countries. Counting the EU's own contributions and those of its member states together, the EU is the largest aid donor in the world.

The EU's aid has previously been criticised by the eurosceptic think-tank Open Europe for being inefficient, mis-targeted and linked to economic objectives. Furthermore, some charities have claimed European governments have inflated the amount they have spent on aid by incorrectly including money spent on debt relief, foreign students, and refugees. Under the de-inflated figures, the EU as a whole did not reach its internal aid target in 2006 and is expected not to reach the international target of 0.7% of gross national income until 2015. However, four countries have reached that target, most notably Sweden, Luxembourg, the Netherlands and Denmark. In 2005 EU aid was 0.34% of the GNP which was higher than that of either the

United States or Japan. The current commissioner for aid, Louis Michel, has called for aid to be delivered more rapidly, to greater effect, and on humanitarian principles.

Regional Development

There are substantial economical disparities across the EU. Even corrected for purchasing power, the difference between the richest and poorest regions (NUTS-2 and NUTS-3 of the Nomenclature of Territorial Units for Statistics) is about a factor of ten. On the high end Frankfurt has €71,476 PPP per capita, Paris €68,989, and Inner London €67,798, while the three poorest NUTS, all in Romania, are Vaslui County with €3,690 PPP per capita, Botoani County with €4,115, and Giurgiu County with €4,277. Compared to the EU average, the United States GDP per capita is 35% higher and the Japanese GDP per capita is approximately 15% higher.

There are a number of Structural Funds and Cohesion Funds to support development of underdeveloped regions of the EU. Such regions are primarily located in the new member states of East-Central Europe. Several funds provide emergency aid, support for candidate members to transform their country to conform to the EU's standard (Phare, ISPA, and SAPARD), and support to the former USSR Commonwealth of Independent States (TACIS). TACIS has now become part of the worldwide Europe Aid programme. The EU Seventh Framework Programme (FP7) sponsors research conducted by consortia from all EU members to work towards a single European Research Area.

VI. CSCAP

The Council for Security Cooperation in the Asia-Pacific (CSCAP) is a "non-governmental (second track) process for dialogue on security issues in Asia Pacific." There are currently twenty member committees of CSCAP (from

Australia, Cambodia, Canada, the European Union, India, Indonesia, Japan, Malaysia, Mongolia, New Zealand, North Korea, Papua New Guinea, the People's Republic of China, the Philippines, Russia, Singapore, South Korea, Thailand, the United States of America, and Vietnam) and one observer (from the Pacific Islands Forum).

VII. GUAM

The GUAM Organization for Democracy and Economic Development is a regional organization of four post-Soviet states: Georgia, Ukraine, Azerbaijan, and Moldova.

GUAM's charter was signed during a summit in Yalta on June 6 to June 7, 2001 by the four current members and Uzbekistan, which later withdrew. According to the current Ukrainian President Victor Yushchenko the charter set objectives for cooperation, such as promoting democratic values, ensuring stable development, enhancing international and regional security and stepping up European integration. Critics point out that only Georgia and Ukraine have shown a deep commitment to democratic values.

Moldova's 2000 elections were won by the Party of Communists of the Republic of Moldova who have, according to the same critics, realigned their foreign policy towards Europe shortly before the parliamentary election held in March 2005. Given the existence of the Russian-led Commonwealth of Independent States (CIS), in Russia GUAM is sometimes seen as a way of countering the Russian influence in the area, and as part of a strategy backed by the United States. However, GUAM leaders repeatedly and officially dismiss such claims and declare their strong willingness to develop close friendly relations with Russia. Moreover, Azerbaijan, the group's main energy power, has managed to avoid any conflicts with Russia in recent years.

Organizational Structure

GUAM is organized as follows:

- An annual meeting occurs between the Presidents of GUAM member states in Yalta, Ukraine. This is considered the supreme body of the organization.
- The executive body is the Council of Ministers for Foreign Affairs of the GUAM states.
- The working body is the Committee of National Coordinators (CNC) consisting of one coordinator from each GUAM member state.
- The Headquarters of GUAM were opened on February 26, 2009 in Kiev, Ukraine.
- There are eight working groups, for the following topics: power engineering; transport; trade and economics; information science and telecommunications; culture; science and education; tourism; the struggle against terrorism, organized crime and dissemination of drugs.

Cooperation between Georgia, Ukraine, Azerbaijan, and Moldova started with the GUAM consultative forum, established on October 10, 1997, in Strasbourg and named after the initial letters of each of those countries. In 1999, the organisation was renamed GUUAM due to the membership of Uzbekistan. A summit in Yalta on June 6 to June 7, 2001, was accompanied by the signing of GUUAM's charter which formalized the organization. However in 2002, Uzbekistan announced that it planned to withdraw from the organization, and following this announcement started to ignore GUUAM summits and meetings.

On May 24, 2005, shortly after the Andijan massacre, Uzbekistan finally gave an official notice of withdrawal from the organization to the Moldovan presidency, thus changing the group's name back to GUAM. In the years following the signing of its charter the grouping was generally considered to have stagnated: Among other things, the 2004 meeting in Yalta was only attended by two of the five leaders while the GUUAM official website still showed the old Georgian flag and listed Uzbekistan as a member.

A summit of GUUAM took place in Chiinau, Moldova, on April 22, 2005. The president of Uzbekistan, Islom Karimov failed to attend, as did the president of Poland, Aleksander Kwaœniewski, who had been invited as an observer. The president of Romania, Traian Basescu, and of Lithuania, Valdas Adamkus, both participated as observers, as did the US Department of State special representative for Eurasian conflicts, Steven Mann, and the OSCE Secretary General Jan Kubis.

The Russian ambassador in Chiºinãu criticized the fact that Russia was not invited to attend. Ilham Aliyev, the president of Azerbaijan, said after the summit: "Our organization is emerging as a powerful force, participating in resolving problems in the Caspian-Black Sea region" while the president of Ukraine, Victor Yushchenko, said that a new page had been written in the history of the organization. In May 22 to May 23, 2006, Ukraine and Azerbaijan announced plans to further increase the GUAM member relations by renaming the organization *GUAM Organization for Democracy and Economic Development* and establishing its headquarters in the Ukrainian capital. Azerbaijani president Ilham Aliyev was to be elected as the first secretary general of the organization. The other members said this was a remarkable step and development. The summit participants were also expected to adopt GUAM by-laws, a declaration and a communique. On May 30, 2006 the Ukrainian Defence Ministry announced plans to establish GUAM peacekeeping forces. On June 19, 2007, presidents of Lithuania, Poland and Romania joined the leaders of GUAM member states at the GUAM summit in Baku, Azerbaijan. Participating at the summit were also the Vice-President of Bulgaria, Vice-Speaker of Estonian parliament, Minister of Economy of Latvia, and the high-level representatives of the United States, Japan, OSCE, the Organization of the Black Sea Economic Cooperation (BSEC), UNESCO, and heads of diplomatic missions accredited in Azerbaijan.

Issues

On April 21, 2005, the GUAM countries formed a common front on several issues in the CIS Foreign Ministers Council that was held at that time in Moscow. Ukraine, Georgia and Moldova lodged complaints against restriction imposed by Russia against some of their national products. At the same time, the four GUAM countries made a proposal to discuss the "frozen conflicts" of Transnistria, Abkhazia, South Ossetia (which remain under de facto Russian military control) and Nagorno-Karabakh. Lastly the other three GUAM nations supported Ukraine's proposal to condemn the Holodomor, the 1930s famine in Ukraine, as a genocide.

Another of the issues associated with GUAM is competition between two proposed transportation corridors to better link Europe with Asia. Russia, Azerbaijan, and Iran have already been through rounds of negotiation on their plan, the North-South Transportation Corridor (INSTC); neighbouring countries (formerly, but no longer with the understandable exception of Armenia) have expressed enthusiasm as well. This corridor would travel along the border between Russia and the Baltic states of the European Union, then continue south through Ukraine. The United States would prefer the critical transportation corridor bypass both Russia and Iran. The plan proposed to GUAM by the United States crosses both the Black Sea and the Caspian Sea. Maritime Security Regimes are codes and conventions of behaviour agreed upon by coastal states to provide a degree of security in territorial waters and on the high seas.

VIII. UNCLOS

One of the best known International Maritime Regimes is the United Nations Convention on the Law of the Sea, or UNCLOS. While UNCLOS is only one of many regimes, or sets of rules, laws, codes and conventions that have been created to regulate the activities of private, commercial and military users of our seas and oceans, it provides the framework for further maritime security cooperation. Most maritime regimes, including UNCLOS, have been created through the United Nations International Maritime Organisation (IMO) in consultation with its member states, and refer to navigation, resource allocation and ownership, prevention of pollution and environmental protection.

To date, the United States is the only state not to ratify UNCLOS but it does adhere to its conventions, and has been the driving force behind current maritime security initiatives, including the Agreement Concerning Co-operation in Suppressing Illicit Maritime and Air Trafficking in Narcotic Drugs and Psychotropic Substances in the Caribbean Area, shortened to Caribbean Regional Maritime Agreement, or CRA.

Where maritime security regimes can differ from other maritime regimes, is that they are created to enable effective policing beyond the jurisdictional constraints of the territorial sea, which ranges from 3 nautical miles (5.6 km) to 12 nautical miles (22 km) from the high water mark of a coastal state. Complications arise when a navy, coast guard, coastwatch, maritime police force, or other agency wishes to intercept (or 'interdict') vessels suspected of carrying out illegal activities, such as piracy against ships, smuggling or there is potential for an act of terrorism. If a suspect vessel is registered, or 'flagged', with a state other than the state of the pursuing authorities, then in most cases the pursuing authorities must gain the permission of the 'flag' state prior to boarding.

If the suspect vessel crosses into the territorial waters of another state, possibly a third state, which is not the home state of the pursuing authorities, then permission must be sought from the territorial state prior to intercepting or boarding.

However, if a prior agreement has been arranged with one or more coastal states, then this can simplify and speed up the process and can make the difference between suspects being detained or not. If several states within a maritime region (such as the Caribbean Sea or Southeast Asia) can come to agreement on 'hot pursuit' and boarding of suspect vessels, then this will reduce time that must otherwise be spent seeking permission.

UNCLOS, Article 111 states that: "The hot pursuit of a foreign ship may be undertaken when the competent authorities of the coastal State have good reason to believe that the ship has violated the law and regulations of that State. Such pursuit must be commenced when the foreign ship or one of its boats is within the international waters, the archipelagic waters, the territorial sea, or the contiguous zone if the pursuit has not been interrupted.....The right of hot pursuit ceases as soon as the ship pursued enters the territorial sea of its own State or of a third State."

While there is a broad school of thought and considerable academic literature on 'regimes', less is known about Maritime Security Regimes as an academic field, or set of theories in its own right. Another related area that requires further research is Regional Maritime Security Regimes, for while there do exist international regimes such as UNCLOS (1988), SUA (1988), ISPS code (2004) there is a trend toward regionalism in maritime security, and exclusion of a strong hegemony to administer it. The CRA is an example of a comprehensive multilateral regional maritime agreement the CRA arose out of a need to respond to the growing prevalence of drug trafficking through the Caribbean

Sea. Initially bilateral agreements between Caribbean states sought to address the delays that occurred when suspects fled into the territorial sea and beyond the jurisdiction of the United States Coast Guard (USCG). These comprehensive agreements sought, among other things, to allow law enforcement officers of one state to be 'sea-rider' LEDETS aboard vessels of the territorial states to reduce lengthy permission-seeking processes. The CRA refers to existing international convention found within the United Nations Convention Against Illicit Traffic in Narcotic Drugs and Psychotropic Substances (1988).

IX. SHANGHAI COOPERATION ORGANISATION

The Shanghai Cooperation Organisation (SCO) is an intergovernmental mutual-security organisation which was founded in 2001 in Shanghai by the leaders of China, Kazakhstan, Kyrgyzstan, Russia, Tajikistan, and Uzbekistan. Except for Uzbekistan, the other countries had been members of the Shanghai Five, founded in 1996; after the inclusion of Uzbekistan in 2001, the members renamed the organisation.

The Shanghai Five grouping was originally created 26 April, 1996 with the signing of the *Treaty on Deepening Military Trust in Border Regions* in Shanghai by the heads of states of Kazakhstan, the People's Republic of China, Kyrgyzstan, Russia and Tajikistan. 24 April, 1997 the same countries signed the *Treaty on Reduction of Military Forces in Border Regions* in a meeting in Moscow.

Subsequent annual summits of the Shanghai Five group occurred in Almaty (Kazakhstan) in 1998, in Bishkek (Kyrgyzstan) in 1999, and in Dushanbe (Tajikistan) in 2000.

In 2001, the annual summit returned to Shanghai, China. There the five member nations first admitted

Uzbekistan in the Shanghai Five mechanism (thus transforming it into the Shanghai Six).

Then all six heads of state signed on June 15, 2001, the *Declaration of Shanghai Cooperation Organisation*, praising the role played thus far by the Shanghai Five mechanism and aiming to transform it to a higher level of cooperation. In July 2001, Russia and the PRC, the organisation's two leading nations, signed the Treaty of Good-Neighbourliness and Friendly Cooperation. In June 2002, the heads of the SCO member states met in Saint Petersburg, Russia. There they signed the SCO Charter which expounded on the organisation's purposes, principles, structures and form of operation, and established it officially from the point of view of international law.

Structure

The Council of Heads of State is the top decision-making body in the SCO. This council meets at the SCO summits, which are held each year in one of the member states' capital cities. The current Council of Heads of State consists of:

- Kurmanbek Bakiyev (Kyrgyzstan)
- Hu Jintao (People's Republic of China)
- Islom Karimov (Uzbekistan)
- Nursultan Nazarbayev (Kazakhstan)
- Dmitry Medvedev (Russia)
- Emomalii Rahmon (Tajikistan).

The Council of Heads of Government is the second-highest council in the organisation. This council also holds annual summits, at which time members discuss issues of multilateral cooperation. The council also approves the organisation's budget.

The council of Foreign Ministers also hold regular

meetings, where they discuss the current international situation and the SCO's interaction with other international organisations.

As the name suggests, the Council of National Coordinators coordinates the multilateral cooperation of member states within the framework of the SCO's charter.

The Secretariat of the SCO is the primary executive body of the organisation. It serves to implement organisational decisions and decrees, drafts proposed documents (such as declarations and agendas), function as a document depository for the organisation, arranges specific activities within the SCO framework, and promotes and disseminates information about the SCO. It is located in Beijing. The current SCO Secretary-General is Bolat Nurgaliyev of Kazakhstan.

The Regional Anti-Terrorist Structure (RATS), headquartered in Tashkent, Uzbekistan, is a permanent organ of the SCO which serves to promote cooperation of member states against the three evils of terrorism, separatism and extremism. The Head of RATS is elected to a three-year term. Each member state also sends a permanent representative to RATS.

Activities

Cooperation on Security

The SCO is primarily centred on its member nations' Central Asian security-related concerns, often describing the main threats it confronts as being terrorism, separatism and extremism. However evidence is growing that its activities in the area of social development of its member states is increasing fast.

At the June 16-17 2004 SCO summit, held in Tashkent, Uzbekistan, the Regional Antiterrorism Structure (RATS) was established. On 21 April 2006, the SCO announced plans to fight cross-border drug crimes under the counter-terrorism rubric.

Grigory Logninov claimed in April 2006 that the SCO has no plans to become a military bloc; nonetheless he argued that the increased threats of "terrorism, extremism and separatism" make necessary a full-scale involvement of armed forces.

There have been a number of SCO joint military exercises. The first of these was held in 2003, with the first phase taking place in Kazakhstan and the second in China.

On a larger scale, but outside the SCO framework, the first ever joint military exercise between the PRC and Russia, called Peace Mission 2005 started on August 19, 2005. Following their successful completion, Russian officials have begun speaking of India joining such exercises in the future and the SCO taking on a military role.

The joint military exercises in 2007 (known as "Peace Mission 2007") took place in Chelyabinsk Russia, near the Ural Mountains and close to Central Asia, as was agreed upon on April 2006 at a meeting of SCO Defence Ministers. More than 4,000 soldiers participated from China. Air forces and precision-guided weapons were have likely to be used. Russian Defence Minister Sergei Ivanov said that the exercises will be transparent and open to media and the public.

In October 2007, the SCO signed an agreement with the Collective Security Treaty Organisation (CSTO), in the Tajik capital Dushanbe, to broaden cooperation on issues such as security, crime, and drug trafficking. Joint action plans between the two organisations are planned to be signed by early 2008 in Beijing.

Cultural Cooperation

Cultural cooperation also occurs in the SCO framework.

Culture ministers of the SCO met for the first time in Beijing on 12 April 2002, signing a joint statement for continued cooperation. The third meeting of the Culture Ministers took place in Tashkent, Uzbekistan, on 27-28 April 2006.

An SCO Arts Festival and Exhibition was held for the first time during the Astana Summit in 2005. Kazakhstan has also suggested an SCO folk dance festival to take place in 2008, in Astana.

Summits

According to the Charter of the SCO, summits of the Council of Heads of State shall be held annually at alternating venues. The locations of these summits follow the alphabetical order of the member state's name in Russian. The charter also dictates that the Council of Heads of Government (that is, the Prime Ministers) shall meet annually in a place previously decided upon by the council members. The Council of Foreign Ministers is supposed to hold a summit one month before the annual summit of Heads of State. Extraordinary meetings of the Council of Foreign Ministers can be called by any two member states.

Future Membership Possibilities

Currently, the Shanghai Cooperation Organisation does not have an official mechanism for admitting new members. Several states, however, participate as observers, some of whom have expressed interest in becoming full members in the future:

- India currently has observer status in the SCO. SCO members have encouraged India to join the organisation as a full-time member, because they see it as a crucial future strategic partner. Additional factors working in favour of India joining the SCO are its major military presence in Central Asia, its close military ties with several Central Asian countries (especially Tajikistan and Russia) and also its deep interest in the region's energy resources. Factors working against India's joining the SCO as a member include India's persistent military rivalry with fellow SCO-observer Pakistan and its general reluctance to make binding ties to groups that could compromise its strategic independence. India's status as a liberal democracy (Every other country in the SCO is rated as "Not Free" by the international NGO Freedom House, whereas India is rated as "Free") also puts it at odds with the members of the SCO.

- Iran currently has observer status in the organisation, and applied for full membership on 24 March 2008.
- Mongolia became the first country to receive observer status at the 2004 Tashkent Summit. Pakistan, India and Iran received observer status at the 2005 SCO summit in Astana, Kazakhstan on 5 July 2005.
- Pakistan currently has observer status in the SCO. In recent times, Pakistan has tried to improve its relations with Russia. Pakistan also quietly backed Russia in its war against Georgia during the 2008 South Ossetia war. Former Pakistani President Pervez Musharraf argued in favour of Pakistan's qualification to join the organisation as a full member during a joint summit with China in 2006. China said that it would convey Pakistan's desire to all SCO member states. In turn, Musharraf was formally invited to the sixth summit of the SCO to take place in Shanghai in June. The Prime Minister of Pakistan Yousaf Raza Gillani once again argued

in favour of Pakistan qualification to join the organization as a full member.

Pakistan and Iran have been lobbying for full membership, while India and Mongolia have not shown strong interest in becoming official members. Russia's permanent representative in the SCO Secretariat Grigory Longinov has claimed that the enlargement of the SCO is impeded by "an immature mechanism of admission of new members", while Secretary General Zhang Deguang argued that an over-expansion might hinder the intensification of the cooperation.

Dialogue Partner

The position of Dialogue Partner was created in 2008 in accordance with Article 14 of the SCO Charter of 7 June 2002. This article regards Dialogue Partner as a state or an organisation who shares the goals and principles of the SCO and wishes to establish relations of equal mutually beneficial partnership with the Organisation.

Sri Lanka and Belarus were granted dialogue partner status in the Shanghai Cooperation Organisation (SCO) at the group's 2009 summit in Yekaterinburg.

Sri Lanka is located in an extremely strategically valued location in the world. China is currently building a harbor in the Sri Lankan town of Hambantota, widely seen as a naval base Chinese ships re-feeling and protecting its naval interests. Sri Lanka recently defeated the separatist LTTE with the cooperation of Shanghai Cooperation Members China and Russia.

Relations with the West

Although the declaration on the establishment of the Shanghai Cooperation Organisation contained a statement that it "is not an alliance directed against other states and regions and it adheres to the principle of openness", many observers believe that one of the original purposes of the SCO was to serve as a counterbalance to NATO and the United States and in particular to avoid conflicts that would allow the United States to intervene in areas bordering both Russia and China.

And although not a member state, President of the Islamic Republic of Iran Mahmoud Ahmadinejad has used his speeches at the SCO to make verbal attacks against the United States.

The United States applied for observer status in the SCO, but was rejected in 2005.

At the Astana summit in July 2005, with the wars in Afghanistan and Iraq foreshadowing an indefinite presence of U.S. forces in Uzbekistan and Kyrgyzstan, the SCO urged the U.S. to set a timetable for withdrawing its troops from SCO member states. Shortly afterwards, Uzbekistan asked the U.S. to leave the K-2 air base,.

X. SOUTH ASIAN ASSOCIATION FOR REGIONAL COOPERATION

The South Asian Association for Regional Cooperation (SAARC) is an economic and political organization of eight countries in Southern Asia. In terms of population, its sphere of influence is the largest of any regional organization: almost 1.5 billion people, the combined population of its member states. It was established on December 8, 1985 by Bangladesh, Bhutan, Maldives, Nepal, Pakistan, India and Sri Lanka. In April 2007, at the Association's 14th summit, Afghanistan became its eighth member.

In the late 1970s, Bangladeshi President Ziaur Rahman proposed the creation of a trade bloc consisting of South Asian countries. The idea of regional cooperation in South Asia was again mooted in May 1980. The foreign secretaries of the seven countries met for the first time in Colombo in

April 1981. The Committee of the Whole, which met in Colombo in August 1981, identified five broad areas for regional cooperation. New areas of cooperation were added in the following years.

The objectives of the Association as defined in the Charter are:

- to promote the welfare of the people of South Asia and to improve their quality of life;
- to accelerate economic growth, social progress and cultural development in the region and to provide all individuals the opportunity to live in dignity and to realize their full potential;
- to promote and strengthen collective self-reliance among the countries of South Asia;
- to contribute to mutual trust, understanding and appreciation of one another's problems;
- to promote active collaboration and mutual assistance in the economic, social, cultural, technical and scientific fields;
- to strengthen cooperation with other developing countries;
- to strengthen cooperation among themselves in international forums on matters of common interest; and
- to cooperate with international and regional organisations with similar aims and purposes.

The Declaration on South Asian Regional Cooperation was adopted by the Foreign Ministers in 1983 in New Delhi. During the meeting, the Ministers also launched the Integrated Programme of Action (IPA) in nine agreed areas, namely, Agriculture; Rural Development; Telecommunications; Meteorology; Health and Population

Activities; Transport; Postal Services; Science and Technology; and Sports, Arts and Culture. The South Asian Association for Regional Cooperation (SAARC) was established when its Charter was formally adopted on 8 December 1985 by the Heads of State or Government of Bangladesh, Bhutan, India, Maldives, Nepal, Pakistan and Sri Lanka.

Afghanistan was added to the regional grouping at the behest of India on 13 November 2005, and became a member on 3 April 2007. With the addition of Afghanistan, the total number of member states were raised to eight (8). In April 2006, the United States of America and South Korea made formal requests to be granted observer status. The European Union has also indicated interest in being given observer status, and made a formal request for the same to the SAARC Council of Ministers meeting in July 2006. On 2 August 2006 the foreign ministers of the SAARC countries agreed in principle to grant observer status to the US, South Korea and the European Union. On 4 March 2007, Iran requested observer status. Followed shortly by the entrance of Mauritius.

Secretariat

The SAARC Secretariat was established in Kathmandu on 16 January 1987 and was inaugurated by Late King Birendra Bir Bikram Shah of Nepal. It is headed by a Secretary General appointed by the Council of Ministers from Member Countries in alphabetical order for a three-year term. He is assisted by the Professional and the General Services Staff, and also an appropriate number of functional units called Divisions assigned to Directors on deputation from Member States. The Secretariat coordinates and monitors implementation of activities, prepares for and services meetings, and serves as a channel of communication between the Association and its Member States as well as other regional organizations.

The Memorandum of Understanding on the establishment of the Secretariat which was signed by Foreign Ministers of member countries on 17 November 1986 at Bangalore, India contains various clauses concerning the role, structure and administration of the SAARC Secretariat as well as the powers of the Secretary-General.

In several recent meetings the heads of state or government of member states of SAARC have taken some important decisions and bold initiatives to strengthen the organisation and to widen and deepen regional co-operation.

The SAARC Secretariat and Member States observe 8 December as the SAARC Charter Day1..

Political Issues

SAARC has intentionally laid more stress on "core issues" mentioned above rather than more decisive political issues like the Kashmir dispute and the Sri Lankan civil war. However, political dialogue is often conducted on the margins of SAARC meetings. SAARC has also refrained itself from interfering in the internal matters of its member states. During the 12th and 13th SAARC summits, extreme emphasis was laid upon greater cooperation between the SAARC members to fight terrorism.

Free Trade Agreement

Over the years, the SAARC members have expressed their unwillingness on signing a free trade agreement. Though India has several trade pacts with Maldives, Nepal, Bhutan and Sri Lanka, similar trade agreements with Pakistan and Bangladesh have been stalled due to political and economic concerns on both sides.

India has been constructing a barrier across its borders with Bangladesh and Pakistan. In 1993, SAARC countries signed an agreement to gradually lower tariffs within the region, in Dhaka. Eleven years later, at the 12th SAARC

Summit at Islamabad, SAARC countries devised the South Asia Free Trade Agreement which created a framework for the establishment of a free trade area covering 1.4 billion people. This agreement went into force on January 1, 2006. Under this agreement, SAARC members will bring their duties down to 20 per cent by 2007.

Dhaka 2005 Summit

The summit accorded observer status to People's Republic of China, Japan, South Korea and United States of America. The nations also agreed to organize development funds under a single financial institution with a permanent secretariat, that would cover all SAARC programs and also ranging from social, to infrastructure, to economic ones.

Membership

Current Members (Alphabetically):

- Afghanistan
- Bangladesh
- Bhutan
- India
- Maldives
- Nepal
- Pakistan
- Sri Lanka

Observers:

- Australia
- China
- European Union
- Iran
- Japan

- Mauritius
- Myanmar (Burma)
- South Korea
- United States.

XI. UNION OF SOUTH AMERICAN NATIONS

The Union of South American Nations is an intergovernmental union integrating two existing customs unions: Mercosur and the Andean Community of Nations, as part of a continuing process of South American integration. It is modeled on the European Union.

The UNASUR Constitutive Treaty was signed on May 23, 2008, at the Third Summit of Heads of State, held in Brasilia, Brazil, but not as of yet ratified by the required ninth nation. According to the Constitutive Treaty, the Union's headquarters will be located in Quito, Ecuador.

The South American Parliament will be located in Cochabamba, Bolivia, while its bank, the Bank of the South (Dutch: *Bank van het Zuiden*, Portuguese: *Banco do Sul*, Spanish: *Banco del Sur*), will be located in Caracas, Venezuela. The Union's former designation, the South American Community of Nations (Dutch: *Zuid-Amerikaanse Statengemeenschap* (help·info), Portuguese: *Comunidade Sul-Americana de Nacoes*, and Spanish: *Comunidad de Naciones Suramericanas*), abbreviated as CSN, was dropped at the First South American Energy Summit on April 16, 2007

At the Third South American Summit on 8 December 2004, presidents or representatives from 12 South American nations signed the *Cuzco Declaration*, a two-page statement of intent announcing the foundation of the South American Community. Panama and Mexico attended the signing ceremony as observers.

The group announced their intention to model the new community after the European Union including a common currency, parliament, and passport. According to Allan Wagner Tizon, former Secretary General of the Andean Community, a complete union like that of the EU should be possible by 2019.

The mechanics of the new entity came out of the First South American Community of Nations Heads of State Summit, which was held in Brasilia on 29 September–30 September 2005. An important operating condition of UNASUR is that no new institutions will be created in the first phase, so as not to increase bureaucracy, and the community will use the existing institutions belonging to the previous trade blocs.

Structure

At the moment, the provisional structure of the UNASUR is as follows:

- The presidents of each member nation will have an annual meeting, which will be the superior political mandate. The first meeting was in Brasilia (Brazil) on September 29 and September 30, 2005. The second meeting was in Cochabamba (Bolivia) on December 8 and December 9, 2006. The third meeting was held in Brasilia on May 23, 2008.
- The ministers of foreign affairs of each country will meet once every six months. They will formulate concrete proposals of action and of executive decision. The President of the Mercosur's permanent representatives committee and the director of the Mercosur's department, the Andean Community's general secretary, ALADI's general secretary and the permanent secretaries of any institution for regional cooperation and integration, Amazon

Cooperation Treaty Organization among others, will also be present at these meetings.

- A Secretary General would be elected, to establish a permanent secretariat in Quito, Ecuador.
- Sectorial Ministers' meeting will be called upon by the presidents. The meetings will be developed according to Mercosur's and CAN's mechanisms.
- The temporary Presidency will be held for a year and will rotate among the member countries between each UNASUR meeting. According to Decisions Reached in the Political Dialogue (Dutch: *Besluiten Bereikt in de Politieke Dialoog*, Portuguese: *Decisoes Tomadas no Dialogue Politics*, Spanish: *Decisiones Alcanzadas en el Dialogue Politics*), which was signed during the I South American Energy Summit, a general permanent office will be created and this will be hosted in Quito, Ecuador.
- On December 9, 2005 a special commission was established in charge of advancing the process of South American Integration (Dutch: *Commissie ter Stimulering van het Proces van de Zuid-Amerikaanse Integratie*, Portuguese: *Commissa Strategical de Reflexes sobre o Processo de Integrate Sul-americana*, Spanish: *La Comision Strategical de Reflection a cargo de formular propuestas con miras a impulsar el proceso de integration sudamericano en todos sus aspectos*). It consists of 12 members, whose function is to elaborate proposals that will help the process of integration between the South American nations.
- An Executive Commission, which was created by the II CSN meeting, was transformed in the Political Commission or Delegates Council, according to Decisions Reached in the Political Dialogue.

Current Work in Progress

Michael Shifter of the Washington D.C. Inter-American Dialogue called UNASUR a "pipe dream for now", while saying that "economic conditions in the region have never been riper for this sort of integration".

Defence Policy

The *South American Defence Council* (SADC) was proposed by Venezuela and Brazil to serve as a NATO-like mechanism for regional security, promoting military co-operation and regional defence. Colombia initially refused to sign up to the defence council due to its strong military ties it has with the United States through the Plan Colombia. However after reviewing the proposal they decided to join on July 20, 2008. Shortly following the signing by Colombia's President, President of Chile Michelle Bachelet appointed a working group to investigate and draft a plan for the new council. Finally on March 10, 2009, the 12 nation members held its first meeting in Chile of the newly formed council.

Non-participating Territories

The following parts of South America are dependent territories and therefore do not participate:

- French Guiana, which is an overseas department of France and is therefore part of the European Union
- The Falkland Islands and South Georgia and the South Sandwich Islands, which are overseas territories of the United Kingdom, though claimed by Argentina..

On 28 December 2005, Chilean former foreign minister Ignacio Walker proposed that the name of the community be changed to *South American Union*; nevertheless, many members stated to him that proposal had already been rejected to prevent confusion related to its acronym (U.S.A. in comparison to the United States of America).

The name was finally changed on April 16, 2007 to "Union of South American Nations" (Dutch: *Unie van Zuid-Amerikaanse Naties*, Portuguese: *Uniao de Nacoes Sul-Americanas*, Spanish: *Union de Naciones Suramericanas*), abbreviated "UNASUR" in Spanish and "UNASUL" in Portuguese. The new name was jointly agreed by all member states during the first day of meeting at the South American Energy Summit held at Isla Margarita, Venezuela.

REFERENCES

"Trinidad PM meets OECS leaders to discuss unity initiative Trinidad PM meets OECS leaders to discuss unity initiative". Caribbean News Agency (CANA).

"BBC Caribbean News in Brief - OECS considers Venezuela request". http://www.bbc.co.uk/caribbean/news/story/2008/11/081121_nibnov21pm.shtml. Retrieved 2008-11-21.

CIA World Factbook 1992 via the Libraries of the Universities of Missouri-St. Louis - scroll to "Member of" section

Communiqué 39th Meeting of the OECS Authority.

"Grenada PM arrives in Trinidad". Caribbean News Agency (CANA).

"Leaders mum on T&T, OECS plan". *Nation Newspaper*. 2008-10-30. http://www.nationnews.com/life/312418478580604.php. Retrieved 2008-10-30.

"OECS Tourism Ministers End Successful Meeting".

Regional Task Force, The Caribbean Community (CARICOM) Implementation Agency for Crime and Security (IMPACS).

Saba takes next step to acquire OECS membership.

Singh, Rickey (13 June 2010). "A USA-CARIBBEAN 'RENEWAL'?" (in English). *Guyana Chronicle*.

Special Committee approves draft texts on Tokelau, US Virgin Islands...

6

Subregional Agenda for Peace in Central Africa

Though home to first man, African continent has had the history of torture, inhuman brutality and feuds. Once bestowed with rich natural resources gradually this continent is transforming into desert in all sense.

Of late, Central Africa has, had the sad privilege of topping the charts in the hit parade of horrors, human bestiality and poverty, an honour that now appears to belong by right to the African continent. The world media giants, which are so fond of bloody images "made in Africa", have been focusing their spotlights on that legendary part of the continent known as the Great Lakes region. Unfortunately, there have been so many of those reports that, in order to express the unique mix of promises and perils implicit in the current situation in black Africa, many of the eminent participants at a first-ever White House conference on Africa were quick to draw parallels between the situations in South Africa and Rwanda. Anthony Lake, National Security Adviser to President Clinton, seeking to illustrate the two contrasting images, spoke of the enthusiasm that South Africa elicits and the horror of the massacres perpetrated in Rwanda.

Taking up this Manichean image in his recent message

to Africa and to the world on present-day problems in Africa, the Secretary-General of the United Nations concluded by saying that Africa disconcerts us because it is constantly giving us reason to swing from hope to despair. All too often it is the scene of ethnic confrontations and civil wars that compound economic misery and underdevelopment.

While it is representative of the situation in the subregion, Rwanda does not have a monopoly on the perpetration of horrors, or even less so, hostilities in the area concerned. For there is a very real danger that what has happened in Rwanda will be repeated in neighbouring Burundi, and Angola is struggling to overcome the effects of a painful war. The rest of Central Africa continues to be throttled by centrifugal forces that fuel political frustration, economic stagnation and social injustice; all these things are undoubtedly helping to push the prospects for genuine sustainable development in the subregion even further into the future.

Here, more than anywhere else, it is becoming increasingly evident that peace is the vital foundation for the vast process of development.

As the Rwanda tragedy has again demonstrated, now, more than ever, peace must be maintained by mechanisms devised to prevent crises and conflicts. The Rwanda tragedy is typical of the very great challenges to security that exist in the post-cold war period, and in that respect is a test of the ability of the international community, in general, and of African countries, in particular, to implement strategies to contain simmering conflicts before they boil over. The objectives of preventive diplomacy, as defined by the then Secretary-General Boutros Boutros-Ghali in his *Agenda for Peace,* are to prevent new disputes from arising and to ease tensions before they result in open conflict, or, when conflict does break out, to contain it. Preventing crises and conflicts in the subregion by promoting confidence-building, security, disarmament and development is one of the key elements of the mandate of the United Nations Standing Advisory Committee on Security Questions in Central Africa.

This Committee—the first institutional African mechanism for preventive diplomacy, consisting of 11 African States, which was established on 28 May 1992 by the Secretary-General of the United Nations pursuant to General Assembly resolution 46/37 B—will, unfortunately, have been conspicuous by its absence at a time when it might have been expected to give concrete proof of its utility. Unable to draw the international community's attention in time to the disaster of unprecedented apocalyptic proportions, which was brewing in the Great Lakes region, the Committee demonstrated just how sadly lacking it was in creativity and strength at the time of the deployment of the international peacemaking and peace-keeping operations in Rwanda and Burundi. We all know how urgent were the pleas that were emanating from the United Nations and France at that time.

Inreply, a few sporadic appeals for common sense were made to the parties involved in the crisis, issued in the form of press releases that were not widely circulated. Furthermore, none of the large-scale collective measures recommended by member States to deal with the situation—participation in international missions to the countries concerned; missions of solidarity to be sent to Angola, Burundi or Rwanda; missions to the Secretaries-General of the United Nations and the Organization of African Unity (OAU) to discuss the crises and conflicts in the subregion—were ever properly implemented.

Undoubtedly, the promises underlying the above-mentioned commitments evaporated when put to the test, owing to the absence or insufficiency of means, including of genuine political will, to act, on the part of the States in question. These questions call for a brief review of the Committee's mandate and of some of the constraints that may have made it difficult to carry out their mandate.

It must be remembered that to seek to assess the Committee's role solely in the light of its activities relating to the recent crises and conflicts of the subregion would be to disregard to a large degree the significance of the fundamental work carried out within this organ; the results of this work can only be appreciated over time. One such achievement was the initialling on 8 September 1994 in Yaounde of a Non-Aggression Pact that sought to unite the 11 member States of the Economic Community of Central African States (ECCAS). Not to mention the rich prospects created by the establishment by the States concerned within their armed forces of units specializing in peace-keeping operations; the establishment of an inter-State general staff committee for crisis management; the commitment of all States in the subregion to refrain from producing, acquiring or transferring weapons of mass destruction; and so on.

This illustrates how significant a role the Standing Advisory Committee could play in the extensive restoration, building and consolidation of peace that must occur in the Central African region. Consideration should be given to the possibility of introducing *the Agenda for Peace* at the subregional level. The Committee has the capacity to pave the way for this large-scale undertaking that should transform Central Africa into a zone of lasting peace, security and development.

This is far from being wishful thinking since, as we

shall see further on, that is central to the global initiative of which the Committee is a part.

The idea of establishing an advisory committee on security questions in Central Africa was first raised on 28 November 1983 at the forty-first session of the United Nations General Assembly by the delegation of Cameroon. At that time, Cameroon, which occupied the chair of the Economic Community of Central African States, proposed the adoption of a series of measures to build confidence and promote security and development in the subregion, and requested the assistance of the United Nations to implement them.

In fact, the formal announcement by the Secretary-General of the United Nations on 28 May 1992 that the Committee had been established was preceded by the convening of two international meetings: the ECCAS Conference on the Promotion of Confidence, Security and Development at the United Nations Regional Centre for Peace and Disarmament in Africa, in February 1988, at Lome, and a seminar-workshop on conflict resolution, crisis prevention and management for high-level civilian and military officials from ECCAS member States, held in June 1991, at Yaounde.

The establishment of the Standing Advisory Committee under the auspices of the United Nations was one of the major recommendations that emerged from this meeting. Welcoming the initiative taken by the African countries concerned, the General Assembly requested that the Secretary-General establish the body under consideration. As set forth in resolution 46/37 B of 6 December 1991, which constitutes the main legal foundation for the Committee's existence, the latter is aimed at "promoting confidence-building measures at regional and subregional levels in order to ease regional tensions and to further disarmament and non-proliferation measures at regional and subregional levels in Central Africa".

On the basis of this mandate, and with the support of the United Nations, the Committee got down to work immediately.

Coping the Challenges

At the organizational meeting, which was held at the ministerial level, in Yaounde, from 27 to 31 July 1992, the participants (ministers for foreign affairs and/or ministers of defence) established the Committee's rules of procedure and adopted a very ambitious programme of work to be implemented in two main phases. The programme focuses on a series of actions that provide for comprehensive, integrated and dynamic approach to the major challenges that confront the subregion. It covers three areas: peace, sustainable development, democracy and human rights. These three areas are central to the issues that justify joint action by a group of States that have understood that "Peace is a prerequisite to development; democracy is essential if development is to succeed over the long term.... Without peace, there can be no development and there can be no democracy.

Without development, the basis for democracy will be lacking and societies will tend to fall into conflict. And without democracy, no sustainable development can occur; without such development, peace cannot long be maintained."

In his *An Agenda for Development,* Boutros Boutros-Ghali underscored this interdependence by describing the dimensions of development: peace as the foundation of development; the economy as the engine of progress; the environment as a basis for sustainability; justice as a pillar of society; and democracy as good governance. This vision is all the more laudable in that it reflects the situation in the subregion, where the threat to peace and security of States is essentially non-military in origin; here "social injustice and the many woes caused by mismanagement of the State and the iniquity of the international economic order" fuel the social explosions that periodically occur in the subregion.

The Committee's programme of work seeks to execute the now familiar canons of the *Agenda for Peace* by providing for a series of measures focusing on preventive diplomacy, peace-building, peacemaking and peace-keeping.

Some of the following measures of preventive diplomacy were classified as needing to be implemented "during the initial stage of activities": adherence by all States of the subregion to international legal instruments on arms limitation and disarmament; conclusion of a subregional non-aggression pact; establishment of hotlines between heads of State of the subregion and increased meetings between them; organization of regular joint meetings of ministers of defence, of the interior and for foreign affairs, as well as of chiefs of staff of the subregion; establishment and improvement of transparency in military activities, etc. Among others, the following priorities were mentioned under peace-building measures: strengthening and consolidation of the democratization process and promotion of respect for human rights in the subregion; establishment of a crisis-management body in each member State; increased involvement of the people and the media in the pursuit of the ideals of peace, security and development in the subregion; elaboration of specific measures for promoting agreement on a balanced and gradual reduction of the military forces, equipment and budgets of the States of the subregion; and assistance in connection with the restructuring of armies and redeployment of the military.

The initiatives to be undertaken in the area of peacemaking and peace-keeping include the establishment of a standing inter-State general staff for crisis management with a view to setting up a subregional peace-keeping force. As regards training, there are plans to develop cooperation with training institutions specializing in the field of conflict prevention and management of peace-keeping operations, with a view to establishing a subregional centre specializing in training peace-keeping personnel. These were some of the strategic and tactical priorities that the Committee was expected to translate into concrete activities.

Assessment of Performance

When we assess the Committee's performance, we find that it has made a little progress, but that this is offset by many missed opportunities.

Adhered to the Schedule of Meetings

The Committee's first achievement is that it has kept its word and brought together high-level civilian and military experts and ministers of defence and/or foreign affairs of the States of the subregion every six months on average. Those meetings, at which participants consider formal measures to build confidence and strengthen security, provide an opportunity for discussion and the fruitful exchange of views. Dialogue helps States to modify their views, avoid misunderstandings and increase the transparency of their activities. In this case, the members of the Committee regularly exchanged views on concepts ranging from preventive diplomacy to joint defence and, more generally, ways and means of peacefully settling crises and disputes. In addition, the review of the geopolitical and security situation in the subregion, an item that is permanently on the agenda, enables officials to keep one another regularly informed of national issues and to work together to find solutions to shared problems.

That is a significant development in the diplomatic practice of the States concerned: the fact that all parties can more or less freely ask one another how the internal political situation is evolving, without being accused of interference. Thus at its sixth meeting, which took place in Brazzaville in March 1994, the Committee invited the Governments of Rwanda and Burundi to create favourable conditions so as to ensure that refugees would be repatriated and to guarantee their security in their own country; it also noted with satisfaction the significant progress that had been made as regards both the democratization process and as regards the resolution of internal conflicts: the implementation of the Paris accords as far as Gabon was concerned; the holding of a national forum for the culture of peace in the Congo; the adoption and promulgation of a transitional constitution in Zaire; the review of the constitution in Cameroon and the adoption of a new constitution in the Central African Republic and in Equatorial Guinea.

Those meetings have proved so useful that the Committee has expressed the hope that sectoral meetings will be organized. The relevant officials of the various countries (ministers of defence and the interior, chiefs of staff and so forth) have therefore been invited to meet as soon as possible in order to adopt or to harmonize policies for combating the illicit trafficking and proliferation of small arms both within each State and in the subregion.

Concluded Negotiations on the Non-Aggression Pact

Within two years of starting work, the 11 States of the subregion have equipped themselves with a legal instrument, establishing their determination to outlaw aggression. The text of the Non-Aggression Pact was adopted in Libreville and initialled in Yaounde in September 1994. This led the Secretary-General of the United Nations to renew his support for the Committee. Speaking to the Advisory Board on Disarmament Matters in Geneva at its January 1994 session, he said that he was "in full support ... of the work of the Standing Advisory Committee on Security Questions in Central Africa.... Their non-aggression treaty should provide a model of a regional confidence-building measure."

Conducted Studies on Future Activities

In addition, notwithstanding the financial difficulties that they are all facing, member States of the Committee undertook to bear the cost of conducting a number of important studies on: the elaboration of a mutual assistance agreement with respect to defence; the establishment of a model national unit specializing in peace-keeping missions; the typology of crises and conflicts likely to require the intervention of the subregional security mechanism; and a proposal to organize a general staff committee for crisis management in the subregion.

Two of the projects, concerning the typology of crises and the status of national units specializing in peace-keeping operations, were finalized and adopted at the Committee's sixth meeting. Chad, Equatorial Guinea and Zaire have already established those specialized units.

In terms of the sort of achievements mentioned above, the Committee has demonstrated commendable farsightedness. However, even though the agreement among the States of the subregion to renounce the use of force in their relations is rightly considered to represent a significant political change, which deserves the support and encouragement of the entire international community, the Committee has yet to take truly meaningful action in its field of competence. The members of the Committee have themselves recognized this and, at the Libreville meeting, the Committee instructed its Bureau to play a more active and dynamic political role in the future by initiating or associating the Committee with any action designed to promote the peaceful settlement of crises and disputes in the subregion. The Bureau was also called on to undertake missions of solidarity and sympathy to States of the subregion caught in the grip of internal or inter-State crises and conflicts.

Given these early opportunities to demonstrate their ability to discharge their specific responsibilities, the successive Bureaus of the Committee have all largely failed. It was only with great difficulty and tardily that the Committee finally managed to express its indignation (and only in the form of a press release) and to stir consciences in the face of the atrocities committed. The unprecedented human tragedy in Rwanda, a member State, elicited just one or two public communiques from the Bureau of the Committee.

It has proved impossible to organize missions of solidarity to Rwanda, Burundi and Angola, which the Committee has been calling for since the first half of 1994. Accordingly, the recommendations calling for their deployment, which are made at each successive meeting, have become largely symbolic.

Moreover, the Committee has neither sponsored nor initiated any action to assist in the international missions currently under way in the affected countries. Such actions as have been taken have been few and isolated. They included material and financial support from Gabon, the dispatch of military contingents to Rwanda by the Congo and Chad, and the "natural" assistance of Zaire, which, by force of circumstance, has become a place of refuge. Hence there have been repeated appeals to the other States of the subregion to continue to express their solidarity with the

Rwandese people in a practical form, to follow suit, or even to participate actively in UNAVEM III in Angola by making troops available to the United Nations and by continuing to support UNAMIR in Rwanda.

The human tragedies unfolding in the Great Lakes region have at the same time underlined the urgent need to put in place an effective preventive mechanism to forestall the recurrence of such horrors in any country of the subregion and highlighted the difficulties that the Standing Advisory Committee has in playing such a role at this stage of its existence.

The cumbersome decision-making procedures in certain national administrations responsible for the follow-up of the Committee's activities, and the inability of the decision makers concerned to manage crises and conflict situations with the requisite speed and effectiveness, are, to a large extent, responsible for this situation and sometimes make one wonder whether sufficient political will exists.

In defence of the officers, it should be pointed out that there are acute communication difficulties between the various capitals of the subregion, and that these have often impeded the flow of information, thereby preventing the holding of certain planned consultations. It is fair to say, however, that the members of the Committee take very little advantage of the numerous occasions for consultations offered by the many international diplomatic meetings.

A Ray of Hope

One can only hope that the Committee will build on its experience and gradually rise to the challenges posed by the many and varied tasks that it is called upon to tackle in the subregion. There are good grounds for optimism about the Committee's future work. These include, *inter alia,* the effectiveness of certain elements of preventive diplomacy advocated in the Committee's programme of action, the support of the international community for their realization, the refusal by the young people of the subregion to take a fatalistic attitude and, in particular, the clear emergence of national civil societies and public opinion in the subregion that identify with the Committee's concerns. Thanks to the Committee's efforts, the time is ripe for building peace and security in Central Africa.

In order for the Standing Advisory Committee on Security Questions in Central Africa to effectively discharge its mandate in the future, a number of important actions consistent with the concept of preventive diplomacy that justified the Committee's creation must be initiated or consolidated without delay. In the views of many, an effective use of preventive diplomacy would be, in the present context, the least costly and most efficient way to build peace in Africa.

Signature and Ratification of the Non-Aggression Pact

It goes without saying that the signature—still awaited—and entry into force of this important juridical instrument would confirm the political will of the States concerned and strengthen the Committee's credibility. The parties' reiteration in a subregional context of their agreement to renounce the threat or use of force in their relations would have significant political consequences. It is therefore very hard to understand why the States in the subregion continue to postpone giving legal force to the Pact.

It is particularly hard to understand since adoption of additional agreements, notably in the field of mutual assistance, could help to temper the appetite for war of certain other African States that share common frontiers with the member countries of the Committee. Thus, mutually freed from the suspicion and mistrust that are due to the current opacity of their defence doctrines and the lack of transparency in their defence budgets, the countries concerned could better tackle the causes of their internal disputes, which are the commonest and bloodiest category of disputes in the subregion.

For, although there are only a few countries that are currently in, or just emerging from, a state of open civil war, virtually all the other States in the subregion are experiencing low-intensity conflicts or, at the very least, situations of instability. The signing of the pact should be complementary to participation by the States of the subregion in the principal international legal instruments on the limitation of weapons, disarmament, peace and security. With this in mind, it would be highly significant to give particular attention to agreements of immediate practical utility for the subregion.

These include the Convention on prohibitions or restrictions on the use of certain conventional weapons which may be deemed to be excessively injurious or to have indiscriminate effects, to which no State in the subregion is yet party. Here, as elsewhere, it would seem that there is not so much a need to draw up new texts as to get States to become party to those that already exist, and to apply them.

Notably, it might thus be possible to get to learn more about the sort of things that give rise to conflicts, which threaten the cohesion of many States in the subregion, and about their impact on the current and future security and stability of the political society concerned. Establishing a mechanism to promote peace and security in Central Africa thus becomes an urgent necessity.

Mechanism for Peace and Security

The main objective of such a mechanism should be to put in place an early warning system capable of detecting early signs of potential crisis. In Central Africa, as elsewhere, the prevention of crises and conflicts requires a system capable of rapidly and effectively compiling and analyzing economic, social and political data, including data on the internal security situation of each State and of the subregion as a whole.

Before the tragic death of the heads of State of Rwanda and Burundi, in April 1994, few Western decision makers had a proper understanding of the forces opposing each other in this part of Central Africa and thus of the potential for disaster that existed. Had there been an appropriate early warning system in the subregion, it might have brought the tensions to the notice of the international community, which, even if it failed to contain them, clearly could have helped to prevent the full scope of horrors that subsequently took place in the subregion.

Such an early warning system should permit the Committee to identify potential conflict situations as early as possible, to analyze them and to propose peaceful measures to deal effectively with them.

The resources required to make such a promising project operational would still have to be mobilized so that the regionalization of crisis prevention (the Committee is one example of this) does not reflect at the security level the general marginalization of Africa. Both the media and civil society have a critical role to play in ensuring the success of this early warning system and in consolidating the other elements of the Committee's platform for action within the prevailing sociological realities.

Greater Involvement of the Media and the Peoples of the Subregion

The importance of this task, which the Committee itself has recognized as being a priority, is self-evident, especially when one considers the role of the media in easing or exacerbating conflicts and crises. This involvement concerns first and foremost the African media and those of the subregion in particular. African media and journalists are best placed to play a significant role within the framework of an overall crisis prevention and management policy in Africa. The Western media have generally taken an interest in Africa only after a conflict has begun.

Moreover, their treatment of information is superficial and usually has little to do with local concerns and realities. The power of modern instruments of mass communication, such as radio and television, was illustrated with the use of the radio station "Radio Mille Collines" to exacerbate tensions in the Rwandan conflict. Yet it has also served to demonstrate the inverse of that experience, namely, that, "although the media are capable of incitement to hatred and confrontation, they can also be used (...) to teach the different communities of a country how to live together in peace."

The media could thus play a leading role in promoting habits of social peace, peaceful coexistence and democracy, thereby contributing to the development of a culture of peace in the subregion. Initiatives that draw inspiration from such a need could thus easily be pursued within the framework of the culture of peace programme launched by UNESCO in keeping with the recommendations of the *Agenda for Peace.*

Subregional Culture of Peace Programme

Coming in the aftermath of crises, such a programme

would help prevent the recurrence of such crises by creating the conditions for peace both objectively and in the minds of people. Efforts to disarm combatants, restoration of law and order, monitoring of elections and promotion and protection of human rights must be accompanied by the building of peace in people's minds. For there can be no peace without a culture of peace. In fact, actions that might be envisaged in this regard could involve tackling such crucial questions for peace in the subregion as the problem of the demobilization of the military. Today, Angola has only recently finished paying the price for its failure to demobilize, even though demobilization was provided for in the May 1991 Bicesse Accords.

It was precisely because the non-governmental forces still had a strong army that it was completely unrealistic to think that a political solution could be found to the Angolan crisis that followed that country's multi-party elections in September 1992. Although today, thanks to the Lusaka accords of May 1995, the spirit of peace seems once more to be hovering over Angola, the Government's army and the UNITA soldiers still have their weapons in hand. In neighbouring Rwanda there remains the risk of rearmament of Hutu former soldiers and' militias among the Rwandan refugees in Zaire. The culture of war is very much alive.

Demobilization should therefore take account of such diverse aspects as the restructuring of the army and the retraining and reintegration of military personnel into civilian life, so as to ensure that weapons are exchanged for shovels and hoes. The culture of peace concerns not only people but also political authorities at the highest level.

The people's involvement should take the form of an

extension of the role of the social actors in the decision-making process, for building peace in Central Africa requires the emergence of a new form of citizenship in which the people become ever more active and take over increasing responsibility for the major choices taken by society. Establishing the foundations of peace also requires a great deal of participation on the part of the highest State authorities, that is to say, first and foremost, the heads of State and Government of the subregion who, as we all know, play a central role in national political systems. Unfortunately, they do not, as yet, seem to fully appreciate the role that the Committee can play in bringing about change.

We have yet to see real evidence of any political will to turn the Committee into a real instrument for promoting peace, security and development. The experience with the draft Non-Aggression Pact illustrates this, as does the extraordinary lack of interest shown by the highest organ of ECCAS in the Committee's activities. We therefore understand why, reacting to the scant heed paid to its earlier appeals, the Committee went so far—at its session in the first half of 1995—as to urge its bureau "to bring the matter before the current Chairman of ECCAS in order to organize a meeting of heads of State and Government to encourage them to become more involved in the implementation of its programme".

It must be remembered that the absence of such determination at the highest level, even the boldest initiatives by other actors in the new subregional partnership for peace in Central Africa will be doomed to failure. It is therefore imperative that this situation be reversed. Only in that way will the region cease to be just a repository of myths about happiness and peace and cease to feed the illusions of the peoples of Central Africa.

7

Latin America and the Caribbean: Strategic Cooperation

Whoever fears to submit any question to the test of free discussion, loves his own opinion than the truth.

—*Ancient Proverb*

Latin America and the Caribbean Island occupy strategic significance in this sub-region particularly because of proximity to mighty USA as a neighbour. Here in this chapter we will put light on the strategic cooperation and confidence-building in the region.

Though cooperation and confidence-building measures may change with the changing world order, more so in the present era of globalisation, yet these are of perpetual in nature. If designed rationally these may prove instrumental in all over development.

It is apt to mention, that while there is no indication that they have the same priority in all these countries, or that the same opportunities to implement them exist among all the States or various groups of States, both discourse and deeds appear to be motivated by a strong intention to move beyond rhetoric to joint action. At the same time, and because of various difficulties, there is also a desire to proceed slowly, but steadily, towards a distant objective: a

Latin American community of nations. For this it will be necessary to take advantage of every available opportunity to establish different forms of interrelation among the countries in the region.

In fact, economic, political and social crisis that affects practically all the countries of the area, the perceptible advance of other regions in relation to Latin America, the disenchantment with armed conflict that seems to be indicated by the outcome of various recent confrontations, the frustration resulting from the slow pace of the integration processes, the survival of perceptions of hostility and the enormous difficulty of going beyond rhetoric in the search for unity: all these elements give rise to endeavours to change the situation.

It is significant to note that the purpose of these endeavours is to present the concept of confidence-building as a versatile, effective and practical means of promoting regional co-operation, and to show that there are already in Latin America political trends and activities that can be labelled "confidence-building".

There appear to be certain possibilities for increasing the significance of this concept on a regional basis, and for making better use of it in relation to peace, co-operation, the limitation of military expenditures and equipment, and eventually, the design of subsystems of security. It is clear that not all of the area designated "Latin America and the Caribbean" can possibly implement such "confidence-building" measures, at least in a way that would offer the same opportunities to all of its components. The special circumstances in Central America and the Caribbean can make it more difficult, albeit more necessary, to establish such a political and military framework.

In fact, the purpose of confidence-building measures,

or in general of confidence-building, is to make increased security possible. The object is, first of all, to lessen the possibility of conflict and to create the conditions necessary for initiation of the processes of arms limitation and disarmament, or of the reduction of military expenditures, or both. In a broader sense, this also touches upon inter-State relations and the possibility of harmonizing them. This concept, which has been discussed extensively in Europe, is one in which there is growing interest in Latin America. Although it has not participated decisively in the conceptual debate or in substantive political negotiations, this region is not unfamiliar with a certain practice of confidence-building, one that has particular and highly significant characteristics.

It is apt to mention that the concept of "promoting confidence" was specifically mentioned in the Final Act of the Conference on Security and Co-operation in Europe held in Helsinki in 1975. It appears in a section entitled "Document on confidence-building and certain aspects of security and disarmament", which establishes an obligation of prior notification of military manoeuvres involving more than 25,000 troops. The document also mentions the possibility of voluntarily exchanging military observers for the manoeuvres, as well as the voluntary notification of smaller manoeuvres or major military movements.

Long before this, the United States and the Soviet Union had agreed on the establishment of direct communication: in the case of a crisis, in 1963; to prevent "accidental nuclear war", in 1971; and to avoid incidents between naval units, in 1972. At the Vienna Talks on Mutual Reduction of Forces and Armaments and Associated Measures in Central Europe a study was made of systems of "related measures" or "collateral measures" clearly related to confidence-building.

It must be remembered that Paragraph 93 of the Final Document of the Tenth Special Session of the General Assembly of the United Nations, the first special session devoted to disarmament, stipulates that in order to facilitate the process of disarmament "it is necessary to take measures and pursue policies to strengthen international peace and security, and to build confidence among States". The Stockholm Conference introduced provisions of major significance, which could be related to concrete measures for the limitation of military deployment.

Notably, European context, which is characterized by a high level of confrontation featuring troops and military equipment of all types, including nuclear armament, there exist other regional contexts in which the concept of confidence has been treated differently, though not with less significance.

For example, the concept of confidence in Latin America necessarily transcends the military dimension. It is set in a complex network of elements ranging from the regional agreements that established legal principles and norms to diverse areas that include the military as well as the political, economic and social processes of integration and co-operation. Latin America is already bound by disarmament agreements such as the Treaty of Tlatelolco, various agreements relating to the peaceful resolution of conflicts and substantive political declarations such as the Ayacucho Declaration of 1974, which was followed by concrete negotiations.

In the similar vein some agreements regarding diverse forms of co-operation and integration as well as significant military exercises are considered important for the promotion of confidence in the region. Thus, for example, the navies of Brazil and Peru developed a joint medical-dental programme catering without distinction of nationality to the population living along the Amazon.

There are also agreements at various levels between military commanders in the border zones with a view to serving common interests. Exchanges of visits, information and invitations of various types take place in Latin America more frequently than may be generally thought. The question of confidence-building has been examined at some length within the framework of the United Nations. It has been dealt with at three special sessions of the General Assembly devoted to disarmament, as well as at various regular sessions, and more specific work has been done on the subject in the Disarmament Commission.

It must be remembered that there are diverse views on confidence-building. Concerned countries have indicated that confidence is a result of various factors such as: whether or not an arms race exists; the concentration of forces and military equipment, or the relative moderation of troops in the border zones; the historical behaviour of the States involved; types of strategic planning; compliance with international agreements; the disposition of these States towards more, or less, open military policies; the possibilities or difficulties of international co-operation in the domain of economic and social development; and similarity of political approaches.

Remarkably, in some cases, more specific conditions have been included, such as: the agreement on notification prior to major military manoeuvres; agreement not to expand military and political alliances beyond earlier levels; the reaffirmation of the principle of the inadmissibility of territorial acquisitions by force; compliance with past agreements; peaceful resolution of conflicts; non-intervention and non-interference in the internal and external affairs of States; the establishment of a new international economic order; and the signing of a treaty renouncing the use of force in international relations.

The challenges to confidence are many and they vary from one region to another. In any given region they reflect the nature of bilateral relations. The challenges to confidence originate in historical experiences, and a combination of factors including geographical realities, strategic concepts, doctrines, military potential and deployment, perceptions and political systems, and economic and social circumstances. All these factors, which are integrated into dynamic processes made up of both past experiences and expectations for the future and which are conditioned by current perceptions, determine the level of confidence that can be achieved in a specific situation. This level will probably determine the decisions that will in turn feed back into the system permanently, in a positive or negative way.

It is apt to mention that in a complex and diverse world, the challenges to confidence are not the same for all and do not have the same origins. They may come from the possibility of nuclear war or from the possibility of a bilateral conflict; from the concentration of forces and military equipment, or from acts of coercion.

One may be based on ideological-political disagreement; another may be nurtured by underdevelopment and international economic injustice. One may be based on military confrontation at the borders, another on the implementation of policies by States which are not necessarily neighbours, such as terrorism, destabilization and intervention.

Yet another may be motivated by the continued existence of unjust situations, general or specific, all-encompassing or localized, historical or recent. Certain specific kinds of threats to security can be met with "measures"—precise, concrete and specific actions. Other threats require "policies", which rather represent attitudes, perceptions and propositions that translate into a diversity of actions over a considerable period of time.

In common parlance, "Confidence" may be defined as a relationship embodying a firm belief in the trustworthiness of the other party. It involves assurance of the truth or of the factual reality of a situation. Confidence-building implies an increase in trustworthiness. In the international sphere, it is confidence that enables States to conclude that their fundamental rights and interests— independence, sovereignty, territorial integrity and development—are not threatened. It is conducive to constructive policies of peace, co-operation, understanding, good will and dialogue. These considerations can be very similar to those generally formulated in relation to security.

It is significant to note that are two basic components in the concept of confidence. One relates to perception; the other is objective and concerns verifiable and provable facts that confirm or deny the observer's perception. Perception is conditioned by, among other things, the historical experiences fixed in the collective memory of peoples. In the priority area of security, the aim of confidence-building is to increase the possibility of confident prediction of the counterpart's intentions through a satisfactory correlation between declaratory defence policies and concrete military activities.

While confidence-building is not, in itself, intended to alter the correlation of forces—at least initially—its aim is to regulate their use in a way that appears to be non-threatening. Thus confidence-building is not a substitute for arms limitation or disarmament, although it is obvious that few things promote confidence more than appropriate agreements in these fields. This is not meant to imply that proper treatment of the objective and subjective factors mentioned above guarantees confidence and makes it possible to overcome conflicts. Obviously, not all conflicts are rooted in differences in the interpretation of verifiable conditions and situations, or in a lack of convergence in the perception or interpretation of them.

Many conflicts result from contradictory interests, and in such situations the relevance of confidence would be only marginal. In Europe there is a high military concentration of political and ideological systems which perceive themselves to be antagonistic, while in other regions the perception of threats to security depends upon more complex factors, encompassing not only military but political, economic and social dimensions.

In fact, in a narrow concept of security, members of military alliances seem to believe that confidence-building measures are actions of a specific character, fundamentally aimed at removing suspicion in the domain of military strategy, and specifically at avoiding, or limiting, the possibility of a surprise attack.

According to this perception, confidence-building measures are not only distinct from disarmament as such, but also differ from arms limitation or the limitation of military deployment. The classic example would be the notification of military manoeuvres, the intention of which is to avoid the possibility of their being converted into a surprise attack.

Remarkably, there is general agreement, however, on the need to endow the concept with maximum effectiveness. This implies an effort to direct the political actions of States towards an objective that is more specific than general harmony, by giving priority to the direct bearing of the concept on the problem of arms and disarmament. This is important, for failing to do so implies a risk, not only that the concept will not be understood but also that it may be misused.

This risk is not negligible inasmuch as it relates directly to the strengthening of a concept that is essential to a proper attitude on the part of States. Measures not based on solid grounds, on verifiable behaviour, and in general on political will expressed in specific, consistent and meaningful action would be of little value.

Obviously, there are policies that lower confidence, such as those of aggression, domination, arms buildups, and colonialism. In the face of such policies, it would be inappropriate to ignore the significance, in terms of confidence-building, of policies of good-neighbourliness, cooperation or integration. Whereas, on the one hand, in the military and security areas, confidence-building measures aim at preventing violations of international law, thereby protecting the inviolability and sovereignty of States against the use of force, on the other hand, in international relations, there is no general rule that prohibits the use of economic power for political ends.

Nonetheless, it is well known that under the provisions of various agreements—the Charter of the United Nations, the Charter of the Organization of American States, the Charter of Economic Rights and Duties of States, the Declaration on Principles of International Law concerning Friendly Relations and Co-operation among States in accordance with the Charter of the United Nations, the Declaration on the Strengthening of International Security, the Declaration on the Inadmissibility of Intervention and Interference in the Internal Affairs of States—certain uses of economic and political power are illegal. Consequently, there must be a will to examine the ways in which the general principles inhibiting the application of political and economic means, in violation of international law, may be translated into measures to safeguard the rights and interests of developing countries, a will to endeavour to make these measures specific, relevant and verifiable.

In Latin America, confidence-building must be understood in its broader sense, not only because perceived threats to security go beyond the military sphere, but also because in the countries of our region the level of "confidence" that may exist is the result of formal agreement, accepted practices, expressions of political will, and a new awareness of the fact that it is impossible for each State to deal with these issues in a strictly individual and exclusive way. For many years, Latin Americans have put emphasis on their attempt to define their own identity, but for various reasons, including their ties to the United States and Europe, no priority has been given to the elements of problems shared by all countries, and the need to establish joint measures to address these problems has received even less consideration.

Now, however, a change is taking place. The consciousness of shared interests and common concerns was most emphatically expressed by the heads of States members of the Permanent Mechanism for Consultation and Concerted Political Action in the Acapuico Commitment. This document deals with questions of the utmost importance, such as the need for political co-operation, recognition of a community of interest in Latin America and the Caribbean, a shared democratic vocation, an appeal to integration, the position of Latin America on the international scene, regional security, including peace and political and economic vulnerability, the- principles of international law that must govern the relations among countries, zones of peace, and the need to prevent the introduction of nuclear arms into the region.

The heads of State members of the Permanent Mechanism made a commitment to co-ordinate action:

- To encourage initiatives in favour of international disarmament and security;
- To foster mutual trust and our own solutions to the problems and conflicts affecting the region;
- To contribute, through co-operation and consultation, to the defence, strengthening and consolidation of democratic institutions;
- To promote and broaden political dialogue with other States and groups of States, within and outside the region;
- To co-ordinate positions in order to strengthen multilateralism and democracy in international decision-making;
- To promote the establishment of zones of peace and co-operation;
- To encourage processes of integration and co-operation in order to strengthen the autonomy of the region;
- To embark on an active, co-ordinated endeavour to eradicate extreme poverty;
- To reinforce co-operation against drug trafficking and also against terrorism.

It is pertinent to note there has been no lack of significant attempts to promote Latin American co-ordination. We may recall, in particular, the case of the Special Committee on Latin American Co-ordination (CECLA), which in the first half of the 1960s displayed dynamism and imagination in trying to define regional economic interests. There have been other efforts in different fields, but on the whole they have been temporary or have not received political or popular support and have gradually faded away.

As a recent development, in recent times, we have seen the creation of dynamic Latin American institutions, set up to address issues of common interest to the countries. However, there is no single Latin American "political" organization comparable to the Organization of African Unity. Nevertheless, an impressive increase can be seen in the number of mechanisms and institutions of regional co-operation, ranging from political processes of considerable importance for peace and security—such as the Contadora Group and its Support Group for the resolution of the crisis in Central America—to professional associations at the sectoral level.

Besides the above, consideration must be given to economic integration procedures, which show that, despite difficulties, Latin America is capable of designing ambitious projects and agreements to promote cooperation in other fields. A case in point is the Andean Subregional Integration Agreement (the Cartagena Agreement), which generated agreements in the sectors of health, education and culture, labour, communications, agriculture, trade and development funding, and reserves, and gave rise to the establishment of a court of justice, a parliament, an advisory council, and meetings between heads of State.

In fact, the Latin American Economic System (SELA) has been consolidating its institutional capacity and significance as a political-economic regional entity. Various action committees have been established to deal with specific aspects of interest to its members or groups of members. Other agreements accord priority to joint development and conservation efforts, as in the case of the Treaty of the River Plate Basin and the Treaty for Amazonian Co-operation. It has taken the Latin American Parliament two decades to achieve institutional consolidation, but political parties are now showing a desire to join the process through the creation of associations such as the Permanent Conference of Latin American Political Parties (COPPAL).

In fact, the most influential institution to date is the Permanent Mechanism for Consultation and Concerted Political Action (the Group of 8), established in Rio de Janeiro in December 1986 and based on the Contadora Group and its Support Group, although different from them. It was the forum for the aforementioned meeting of eight heads of State in Acapuico in September 1987. Even apart from the substantive Agreement signed on that occasion, the meeting was hailed as a historic occasion: for the first time a group of Presidents of Latin American democracies met to discuss political, economic and security matters of the utmost importance without an invitation from, or participation by, the United States.

It must be remembered that there has been an increase in co-operation among institutions, centres, and professional, educational and research associations. The research associations are promoting an interest in the study of international and Latin American relations from a perspective which challenges confrontational perceptions among the countries and peoples of the region. The regional approach to the arms limitation issues is certainly among the most promising.

In the particular case of Latin America, it would be more appropriate to consider arms limitation as part of a world security system. In practice, however, it has merely served the strategic interests of the dominant Power in the hemisphere. It is usually noted that, in the South American subregional context, threats to security must include: elements such as those contained in the conflict situations in the Malvinas and in Central America; ideological differences as well as differences between political regimes; military presence and extraregional strategies in certain countries; territorial disputes and border tensions; subversion and other forms of internal violence; drug trafficking; and the status of military denuclearization in Latin America.

Besides these, factors such as extreme poverty, scientific and technological backwardness, ambiguous relations between military and civilian sectors, external debt, ecological accidents, and the weight of military expenditures in relation to expenditures in the basic social sectors pose threats to security. The most critical characteristics of the region in the past four decades are the poverty that prevails in most of the countries, the growth of military expenditures, and the increase and sophistication of armaments.

Notably, the first condition for confidence is the conviction that force will not be used in trying to resolve international issues. The use of force would not only violate law and create new sources of tension but, in the case of Latin America and in particular of South America, it would not serve any purpose inasmuch as there do not appear to be any political objectives, no matter how legitimate they may be, that can be resolved by means of force.

Towards Joint Action

It must be remembered that Latin America does not have to specify whether it will adopt a broad or a restricted confidence-building concept. Its historical responsibility is the preservation of peace and the promotion of development and integration, the preservation of its security, and the implementation of the policies required to overcome the conceptual divergences that separate its countries, as well as the implementation of all the measures needed to preclude the possibility of conflict and to promote co-operation, including military co-operation.

To that end, some proposals are set out below, classified where possible by sectors with special responsibilities. Some overlapping is, of course, unavoidable.

A. Military Sector

1. Information

General exchange of publications; possibility of reaching agreements on prior notification of military activities, including movements and manoeuvres, and invitation of military observers;

2. Training

Student exchanges between military schools; preparation of special courses or seminars for foreign and national students on matters of common interest; establishment of courses on disarmament and arms limitation, as well as courses in defence economics, in military schools; participation at various levels of cadets and officials in special activities such as summer courses on rescue at sea, on land and in the air; in medical and sanitary programmes, and in general in as many related activities as possible;

3. Contacts

Increase in the number of official visits and/or military delegations at various levels; establishment of basic procedures in order to avoid incidents, as well as systems for direct communication, including emergency lines and other convenient channels for dealing with accidental situations and misunderstandings; contacts in certain institutional sectors, such as the academic, military, athletic and other areas, with a view to decreasing perceptions of hostility or confrontation; and the organization of military exercises involving only South American countries, as has been done in the past;

4. Institutionalization

Consideration of a periodic South American conference at an appropriate level to manage the activities mentioned above;

B. Political Sector

1. Co-ordination

Political co-ordination at appropriate levels for the handling of matters of common interest, such as external debt; parliamentary participation in scheduled meetings and visits to discuss questions relating to security in the broad sense of the concept, and to promote the limitation of military expenditures and armaments;

2. Reaffirmation of Principles

Individual or joint political reaffirmation of the solemn commitment to peace, the non-use of force in international relations, and the resolution of differences by pacific means;

3. Establishment of Procedures and Projects

Mechanisms of joint action in the struggle against the drug traffic, including procedures for joint police and/or military operations by two or more countries to fight these transnational forms of crime; promotion of the study of new security concepts; inclusion in the platform of political parties of plans for the promotion of peace, security for all, and the limitation of armaments and military expenditures; creation of a programme of co-operation in the event of natural disasters; establishment of government priorities for development projects concerning two or more countries, in particular in border zones; continuation of co-ordination of the mechanisms and opportunities for the implementation of the limitation of military expenditures and for the gradual integration of the military sectors of industry;

C. *Diplomatic Sector*

1. Courses

Creation of courses on disarmament, arms limitation and related subjects in diplomatic schools;

2. Support for Activities

Commitment of the diplomatic missions to celebrate Disarmament Week and support the United Nations World Disarmament Campaign; support of the activities of the United Nations Regional Centre for Peace, Disarmament and Development in Latin America and the Caribbean;

D. *Academic Sector*

1. Courses

Creation of courses on defence economics, arms limitation and disarmament;

2. Research and Studies

Promotion of peace research, studies on disarmament and development, including research on the economics of arms production; studies and research on the relation between democracy in Latin America, arms build-up and external debt;

E. *Civic Sector (Including Non-governmental Organizations, Churches and Media)*

1. Seminars

Periodic seminars on responsibility in the forming and guidance of public opinion in the sphere of democratic security;

2. Support for Activities

Participation of the Latin American media in the United Nations World Disarmament Campaign.

More than half of the Latin American countries have high levels of military expenditure in proportion to GNP. The common element among them is the pre-eminence of the armed forces in the political, economic and social life of the country. Each of them, for different reasons, has experienced a hypertrophying of the military institution within the State and society.

Thus, in Argentina, the armed forces have unexpectedly recovered some institutional autonomy despite the efforts of President Alfonsfn's Administration to curb both military expenditure and the armed forces' political influence in the aftermath of the conflict in the South Atlantic and following the imposition of sanctions for their massive human rights violations—which they resisted. In Chile, as a consequence of long military rule, the armed forces have exercised control and have been a significant presence in the life of the nation. Cuba's extra-continental strategic projection and defensive orientation have given the military considerable weight within the State. The military component is clearly visible in El Salvador, Honduras and Nicaragua, countries engaged in "low-intensity warfare". Guyana is in the process of developing the State and is seeking to progress within a militaristic framework. Panama's relationship with the United States has been the cause of its militarization. In Peru, the critical situation resulting from terrorism has now been added to the traditionally prominent role of the military.

In democratic Uruguay, the military presence is still too large, both politically and socially. These are the countries in which a comparatively greater share of resources is being diverted to defence purposes—both internally and externally—than the respective economies can afford. On the other hand, countries of such diverse size as Brazil and Costa Rica, or with differing internal emergency situations, such as Guatemala or Mexico, richer or poorer, like Colombia or Bolivia, are allocating a smaller part of their gross national product to defence as a result of the armed forces' relatively smaller part in decision-making at the governmental level.

To conclude, it may safely be surmised that military expenditures are basically dependent upon the position of the armed forces in the respective States. Thus, the ability to curb military expenditures and arms supplies in Latin America will depend upon the state, the development and the direction of the domestic system of military and civilian relations' towards more significant civilian control. It is the ruling elite's decisions, made in accordance with the prevailing domestic circumstances, that determine the high level of expenditure or the decision to reduce it. This trend is once again evident in the case of Latin America in those countries where the armed forces play a conspicuous decision-making role.

If we compare import figures for arms and military technology of the countries of the region, we find that Argentina, Cuba, Ecuador, Nicaragua, Peru and Venezuela have been the principal recipients of defence technology in the years 1982-1986, representing 82.6 per cent of total transfers to the region.

This situation may be attributed, first, to the role played by the armed forces within the State, as has been indicated earlier, and secondly to the availability of national resources. Thus, those countries which, compared to the rest of the region, have a relatively high GNP, such as Venezuela, or which have an economic surplus resulting from oil production, such as Ecuador, and which do not have a significant arms industry, are net importers. It may be attributed, thirdly, to the fact that there are countries with a low per capita GDP which are net importers, such as Nicaragua and Peru, as they are facing tensions and conflicts that require military actions.

Cuba may be considered a typical example. In 1984 it combined all three of the above conditions: the armed forces occupied a central position in the political scheme, a large share of the country's resources was allocated to defence, and there was a perceived threat of conflict and confrontation with the United States.

Thus, the role of the armed forces, the economic availability of resources and the presence of conflicts are the principal factors stimulating Latin America's imports of military technology.

It is important to note that the type of weapons being transferred to the region has increasingly modern technological components. It is important to note the differences among suppliers. The United States has somewhat increased the transfer of tanks and self-propelled cannons, all types of aircraft, helicopters and missile launchers. The Europeans have specialized in the sale of personnel carriers, aircraft and missiles. Finally, the USSR has increased its sale of tanks, helicopters, and, notably, anti-aircraft missiles.

The transfers of more sophisticated and combat armaments are limited to a fixed number of military links between the countries of the North and Latin America. Thus, the USSR's clients are Cuba, Nicaragua and Peru. Those of the United States are Mexico, Venezuela, Peru and El Salvador, among many others. France has Argentina, Chile, Ecuador and Peru as its main customers. The United Kingdom had Argentina among its regional clients and now has Chile and Ecuador. The Federal Republic of Germany has four important clients: Argentina, Chile,

Colombia and Peru. Lastly, Italy has Argentina, Ecuador, Peru and Venezuela.

Even though there are many reasons for the growth of the arms industry on the continent, international tensions give rise to a specific response, namely, enhancement of the industry's own capabilities of research, development and arms production. The will of the respective armed forces to acquire, by their own efforts and from resources generated locally, the means for deterrence and defence is thus reinforced. This reflex action of self-sufficiency serves as an added stimulant to all other contributing factors, and together they explain the history of the creation and development of the local arms industries.

This decision is bolstered by the growth of a non-military industrial plant already in place, which in turn affects and determines the limits that the respective military industries must observe in their development. An analysis of several countries which currently have a military industry of some importance will illustrate these statements.

Argentina is one of the Latin American countries that has shown military industrial activity over a number of years. The first decisions to manufacture weapons date from 1920. However, the Direccion General de Fabricas Militares (DGFM), established in 1941, strengthened government activity in this sector by linking it to the overall industrial effort. From 1945, the DGFM co-ordinated the manufacture of arms of all of the armed forces. In this regard, the air force, with the assistance of German engineers, began the design and manufacture of planes such as fighter-bomber and transport aircraft. Their production began in 1956. Likewise, the navy has designed and built vessels since 1938 at the Rio Santiago shipyards, where patrol boats and frigates were later built.

The army, with German assistance, produced heavy artillery, machine-guns and various types of ammunition. In 1940, the Rosario plant developed and manufactured a series of machine-guns, which are still in use today. With the initial impetus provided through German collaboration, a relatively modest research and development (R and D) entity was established, which was able, to supply the military industry. Although no more than 1 per cent of the GNP was ever allocated for R and D, from 1958 the Consejo de Investigaciones Cientificas y Technologicas was the principal source of subsidies for this kind of research. Likewise, the Institute Nacional de Tecnologfa Industrial, the Comision Nacional de Energia Atomica and the Comision Nacional de Investigaciones Espaciales have made the development of Argentina's military and nuclear industry possible and, with the help of foreign technical assistance, this industry is among the largest in Latin America. R and D activities have been linked to the industrial sector, encouraging the development of the State steel, aluminium and motor vehicle industries.

Together with the DGFM, the Direccion Nacional de Industria e Investigaciones Aeronauticas designs and manufactures aircraft equipment under Air Force supervision. While it attempted to produce combat planes in the 1950s, in the 1970s manufacture concentrated on the production of transport and counter-insurgency aircraft such as the IA-50 Guaranf II and the IA-58 Pucara models. This has led to the design of combat aircraft such as the IA-60 Pucara fighter and a helicopter, the "Cicare CH-11 Colibri." DGFM itself has produced civil aircraft and assembled the French AMX-13 tank. Argentina is developing light and medium-sized tanks and armoured personnel carriers under a co-production agreement with the firm of Thyssen-Henschel of the Federal Republic of Germany. The government shipyards, Astilleros y Fabricaciones

Navales Estatales, have the capacity to produce locally designed naval equipment such as frigates and missile launch boats.

They also arm submarines with parts provided by the Federal Republic of Germany. All this domestic R and D activity has led to co-production agreements with extra-continental firms, which offer excellent prospects for the development of the Argentinian military industry. For example, it planned to build a training jet of limited capacity for tactical support missions in collaboration with the German firm of Dornier. This plane would be manufactured by the Direccion Nacional de Industrias e Investigaciones Aeronauticas in the province of Cordoba. This aircraft, designated the "LA-63", was mass-produced in 1985. With the support of its own R and D facilities, the Argentinian military industry has the capacity to raise its technological level, and it would not be surprising to see the co-production agreements for aircraft and tanks followed by agreements with Spain to construct ships, with the Federal Republic of Germany for submarines, and with France for coastal craft.

The Argentinian example shows the extent to which its military industry was stimulated by increased tensions with the United States and the circumstances of its isolation on the international scene. The impetus given to the military industry during the Second World War was maintained in the post-war period as a result of the politics of Peronist populism in its first phase. Later, and especially during the rule of General Videla, Argentina developed its military industry in political isolation from the United States as a result of the attitude taken by the Carter Administration in respect of human rights. This last period, of course, coincided with the heightening of tension with Chile in the Beagle zone. However, Argentina provides for its own defence needs by stimulating and supporting the local manufacture of arms. Although it has complemented these manufactures with substantial purchases abroad, amounting to $US 210 million in 1978, local production of light and heavy weapons nevertheless became one of the pillars of its defence policy. The manufacture of the Condor II medium-range missile is a case in point.

The Brazilian aeronautical industry is another example of the way in which the expansion of the local arms industry was helped by adverse international conditions. Towards the end of the 1970s, Brazil was still unable to resume its international alliances. This is clearly seen in the arms import figures, which went from $US 18 million in 1966 to $US 70 million in 1969. The response to that situation was the development of what is today Brazil's strongest industry, its aeronautical industry. On 19 August 1969, the President signed a decree establishing the Empresa Brasilena de Aeronautica (EMBRAER) (Brazilian Aeronautical Company), which began its activities in January 1970. This represented the culmination of Brazil's effort to develop its own technology in the military and civil aviation sector. Indeed, in 1965, the Institute de Investigacion y Desarrollo del Departamento de Aviacion (the Aviation Department's Research and Development Institute) decided to replace the old "Beech C-45" of the Brazilian Air Force.

For this purpose, the Centro Tecnico de Aeronautica (Technical Centre for Aeronautics) (now the Centro Tecnico Aeroespacial (Technical Center for Aero-space)) requested the assistance of the French engineer Max Holste and decided to re-equip the air force's "North American T-6", a project later abandoned. The replacement of the "C-45" was effected with the development of the twin turbo-prop "IPD-6504", which later became the "EMB-100". Development of this plane began in June 1965 and the first prototype was built in 1966. Outfitted with Pratt &

Whitney PT-6 engines, its first flight occurred on 26 October 1968. The Brazilian Air Force ordered 80 of the EMB-110 Bandeirante version.

This achievement of the military aeronautical industry made it possible for EMBRAER to develop civilian aircraft such as the EMB-200 Ipanema for agricultural use. It made its first flight in July 1970 and five versions were built, amounting to a total of 400 units. Between 1973 and 1974 the energy crisis forced Brazil to develop its aeronautical industry more aggressively and, under contract with Piper, five different types of one and two-engine planes were produced. The modified version of the Bandeirante alone—the EMB-110P—was extremely popular with local airlines and air forces in and outside the region.

In 1976 EMBRAER developed three versions of the Bandeirante: the Kl, for military use; PI, a modified civilian version of the Kl; and the P2, strictly for passengers. Orders for the last three models were obtained from American, British and other foreign airlines. The Brazilian aeronautical industry is supported by the Centro Tecnico Aeroespacial, around which are grouped the institutes of Tecnologia Espacial, Investigacion y Desarrollo and Investigaciones Aeroespaciales (Space Technology, Research and Development, and Aerospace Research).

The Centre, a collaborating entity of EMBRAER, permits the use of aerodynamic tunnels and physical laboratory experiments. As a result of these developments, EMBRAER meets the needs of the Brazilian Air Force in the following areas: basic trainers with capacity for ground attack; twin turbo-props, pressurized or unpressurized, for personnel and utility transport; maritime patrol aircraft, search and rescue aircraft, and special photogrammetric and calibration types. With the installation of these capacities, EMBRAER functions as a sub-contractor and co-producer.

The Chilean example also serves to corroborate our statements. From 1973, its military Government encountered serious difficulties in obtaining arms supplies. The situation became more acute with the increasing tensions in the north with Peru and with Argentina in the Beagle zone. While the first tensions tended to disappear, the second increased steadily. In 1976 Chile earmarked $US 120 million for arms imports, pushing military expenditure beyond the limits required for economic stability. From then on, in an international climate hostile to the regime, the armed forces encouraged the development of a local arms industry, contradicting all the economic postulates of the regime.

These stated that without an industrial base, Chile would be reduced to the status of net importer of such products. Nevertheless, the needs arising from international isolation and the traditional State-oriented ideology of the Chilean armed forces resulted in a substantial effort of "arms import substitution". Chile had a limited production capacity and did not export military equipment. It produced the 7.62 mm FN-FAL rifle and a heavy 7.62 mm FN machine-gun. All other rifles, machine-guns, sub-machine-guns, anti-aircraft cannon, mortars, recoil-less rifles and howitzers were manufactured in Denmark, France, the Federal Republic of Germany, Switzerland and the United States. Likewise, naval equipment was imported, whereas the air force and the navy had the capacity to maintain and repair aeronautical and naval equipment.

Thus, while Chile was a net importer, it possessed the minimum capability required to develop a larger military industry. This was made possible as a result of the particular domestic and international political conditions it has faced over the past seven years. In 1960, Astilleros y Maestranzas de la Armada (ASMAR), the navy's shipyards, were established as an independent governmental entity, and are now able to repair warships, merchant ships, fishing vessels and factory ships. ASMAR is also able to build ships and landing craft of up to 50,000 tons and oil exploration rigs. ASMAR currently employs 4,500 people, including electronic engineers and naval propulsion technicians. It also has its own foundry and laboratories. The Navy, within the framework of its collaboration with France, began manufacturing under licence two BATRAL landing craft (light transport craft) with capacity to transport an infantry company, five combat vehicles and other equipment. BATRAL is equipped with two 40 mm cannons, two 81 mm mortars and a helicopter landing-track.

Las Fabricas y Maestranws del Ejercito (FAMAE) (the Army's factories), the Logistics Air Command and a private firm, Sociedad General de Comercio (SOGECO), jointly developed a high-precision machine-gun. This weapon, designated "Crane One", includes a carrier which is connected to a vehicle, has two 20 mm tubes, and fires nearly 1,000 projectiles per minute. A similar agreement was made between the army and a private firm in 1978 "when the Chilean Government ordered some private firms to produce weapons as a means to circumvent the freeze imposed by the traditional suppliers". Cardoen, an explosives plant, is currently manufacturing "Mowag" armoured cars "under Swiss licence, for the transport of troops and to support combat action once they are equipped with light armament." The air force, for its part, has assembled the first Mirage 50 purchased from France and has gone on to build a Piper Dakota plane wholly armed domestically, with 50 per cent of the parts from the United States, a percentage which will be reduced in the years to come.

This aircraft, used for instrument flight training and liaison, will prepare the way for a more ambitious project, namely, the manufacture of the Spanish Avio-jet CASA-

101 jet aircraft for advanced training and combat. These developments demonstrate that, in response to the chronic international political situation originating-in 1973, the Chilean armed forces have given priority to their own arms research, development and production. Lastly, the example of the budding Mexican military industry serves to demonstrate the connection between problems deriving from the new international situation, hemispheric alliances and the armaments industry itself. Mexico has made rapid progress in the development of its local arms industry. It is now able to manufacture armoured vehicles through Diesel Nacional (DINA), a State-controlled enterprise, and is striving to manufacture the HK-53 sub-machine-gun assault rifles for the Army. It is building corvettes of the Aguila type and Azteca patrol boats.

The Mexican Government is encouraging the development of its own scientific and technological research capability, which will in time establish close links with the growing Mexican arms industry. The Consejo Nacional de Ciencias y Tecnologfa (the National Council for Science and Technology) has made various plans for the development of the country's scientific and technological capability. It is interesting to note that for the period 1978-1982 a third of the funds allocated went to the industrial sector for projects directly related to military use, such as those directly connected to the chemical industry; telecommunications; transport; metallurgy, ferrous and non-ferrous; electronics; metal works; the motor vehicle industry; instruments, and investments in technology. The Ministry of National Defence is among those which are deeply interested in obtaining funds for these purposes.

These facts explain why the Mexican industry is competent to plan the co-production of the Argentinian TAM tank in the near future. Likewise, according to international sources, Mexico is planning to produce under licence the Brazilian counter-insurgency aircraft EMB-326 Xavante and the EMB-110 transport. The same sources state that there is a licensing agreement with Israel to co-produce the Arava aircraft. These warlike developments in a country hitherto committed to continental disarmament demonstrate how important political factors, such as the exploitation of Mexico's huge oil riches, have helped to bend an intransigent pro-disarmament posture in favour of a local armament industry. These examples, presented in brief, show that the military industry has developed in Latin America in the last few years as a specific response to problems with which the countries are confronted in their international relations in general, and at the hemispheric level in particular.

The development of the Mexican military industry arises from the particular character of its relations with the United States, which lead it to seek some autonomy with respect to its arms supplies. In the cases of Argentina, Brazil and Chile, there is a demonstrable link between the effects of international isolation and the decision to increase the capacity of the local war industry. This is what is taking place rather than the strengthening of a process by which conflicts are resolved by peaceful means.

Despite the obvious link between the development of local armaments industries and the vagaries of international relations, this is valid only as long as the conditions under which it originated continue to exist. While afterwards these industries may become a source of foreign currency savings and substitution of war material imports, they jeopardize the future use of an important proportion of tax resources and are not an adequate response to new international circumstances. As a consequence, it is legitimate to question these diversions and their medium-

and long-range effects on the allocation of tax resources. In Chile, for example, the Fabrica Nacional de Aeronaves (FANAVE) (National Aircraft Factory), founded in 1953 and closed down in 1960 for purely commercial reasons, is a case in point. While its establishment was encouraged in the context of that Administration's industrial policy, its economic viability became a valid argument for the subsequent Administration. The latter operated in a framework of international relations in which the supplying of the armed forces did not present major problems. With the armed forces subjected to civilian rule, alternative cost criteria became a primary consideration and the idea was abandoned.

This example shows that, while the impetus to create an arms industry is assisted in various ways distinct to the international situation, its development possibilities are dependent upon the external framework in which it operates and the possible alternative uses of such resources. This is a crucial factor, and one which calls into question the development of the arms industry in the countries of the region.

To the extent that defence capabilities are closely related to a country's ability to establish international alliances, the problem of national defence appears fundamentally to be a political issue. Nevertheless, in conditions of isolation a need for self-sufficiency arises, which in turn entails future financial commitment. Thus, to the extent that the international circumstances of the region's countries are temporary, the creation and development of a local armaments industry jeopardize resources which might later meet domestic needs.

Leaving aside the political problem implied in the formulation of development objectives and goals, and once the moment of international "emergency" has passed, the principal limitations of the arms industry become evident.

First of all, there is the economic problem of developing an industry that operates at much higher technological levels than the national "technological average". This disparity results in a lack of "pull" of this more modern sector with regard to the whole national industrial sector, which lags behind and is unable to profit from the investment. The arms industry generates few demands on the overall economy and has no other sub-products to offer; its workers are highly specialized, and inputs are produced locally only in part. Thus, the industrial war industry withdraws active resources from one sector and allocates them to others which, dynamic as they are, have no effect on the rest of the economy in terms of technology.

Secondly, even though a local military industry is highly profitable and productive, it is based originally on a country's high military spending. Subsequently, the industry may focus on export, but it will continue to depend largely on the local armed forces' consumption, which was the reason for its creation in the first place.

Lastly, the development of a military industry does not present the same characteristics as an industrialization process based on import substitution. To the extent that defence activities consume capital that would otherwise be available at the local level, such expenditures affect national productivity as a whole, both economically and ideologically. In relieving a relative capital glut through the development of a local defence industry made solvent by high military expenditure, basic political imbalances are obscured and the means of correcting them are confused.

Thus, defence spending used to maintain a local military industry helps obscure social disparities and the unequal distribution of resources. To the extent that military spending for this industrial effort is presented as an urgent and immediate national task, it justifies the fact that existing economic resources for public investment in industry are not used to meet basic needs. This leads to the creation of a socio-economic structure which allows investment in areas that supply those sectors that constitute an effective market, that is, the high-income and luxury-oriented market. Such available capital can be created only in a more egalitarian socio-economic environment, oriented towards the satisfaction of the basic needs of the majority of the population.

To sum up, the military industry in Latin America has arisen as a consequence of international conditions resulting from exceptional political situations and its development enhances the unequal domestic social conditions characteristic of the region.

8

Disarmament: Significance and Relevance

> A man's delight in looking forward to and hoping for some particular satisfaction is a part of the plea-sure flowing out of it, enjoyed in advance. But this is afterward deducted, for the more we look forward to anything the less we enjoy it when it comes.
>
> —*Arthur Schopenhauer*

In the present day globalised world order, when we have everything global, peace and security are still endangered. Though cold war rivalry has come to cool, United States of America has emerged as sole super power, yet its recent attitude and activities have been instigating new sort of arms race. Many so called developing countries are in the race of obtaining latest nuclear power and missile technologies—thus posing threat to world peace and human survival.

Here in this chapter we will take the issue of disarmament and its significance for security and development.

Since its foundation, the United Nations has made the goals of multilateral disarmament and arms limitation central issues in the maintenance of international peace and security. Highest priority has been given to the reduction and eventual elimination of the weapons of mass destruction, which have posed the greatest threat to humankind.

While the objective of reducing the threat of nuclear, chemical and biological weapons remained constant through the years, the scope of the deliberations and negotiations on disarmament has changed, reflecting the evolving political realities and international conditions. In the post-cold-war period, the international community has begun to consider more closely the threats related to the excessive and destabilizing accumulation of conventional armaments, the proliferation of small arms and light weapons, and the humanitarian crisis caused by the massive deployment of landmines in conflict areas.

Role of United Nations

In fact, United Nations machinery for disarmament was established by the Charter and subsequent decisions of the General Assembly. The Charter has given the General Assembly the chief responsibility of considering "the general principles of cooperation in the maintenance of international peace and security, including the principles governing disarmament and the regulation of armaments" (article 11).

The Assembly has two subsidiary bodies dealing with disarmament issues, open to all Member States: the *Disarmament and International Security Committee* (the First Committee), which meets during the regular session and deals with all disarmament issues on the agenda of the Assembly; and the *United Nations Disarmament Commission,* a specialized deliberative body that focuses on specific issues, such as the creation of nuclear-weapon-free zones and guidelines for international arms transfers. The General Assembly held special sessions on disarmament in 1978, 1982 and 1988. The Conference on Disarmament is the international community's single multilateral negotiating forum for disarmament agreements. This body, working strictly on the basis of consensus in matters that touch the national security interests of States, has a limited membership, expanded in 1996 from 38 to 61, and a unique relationship with the General Assembly. It defines its own rules and develops its own agenda, but takes into account the recommendations of the Assembly and reports to it annually. Most recently, the Conference successfully negotiated both the *Chemical Weapons Convention* (1993) and the *Comprehensive Nuclear-Test-Ban Treaty* (1996).

In the United Nations Secretariat, the Department for Disarmament Affairs implements the decisions of the Assembly in matters of disarmament. Its responsibilities include maintaining and operating the Register of Conventional Arms, exchanging information called for in various arms agreements, facilitating the discussion of disarmament issues in the General Assembly and the Conference on Disarmament, and supplying impartial information for educational purposes in pursuit of the goals of the Organization in this field.

The United Nations Institute on Disarmament Research (UNIDIR), based in Geneva, undertakes research on disarmament and related problems, particularly international security.

Current Scenario

It is pertinent to note that the sweeping political changes of recent years have led to important achievements in multilateral disarmament, some of which had been sought for decades, such as the culmination of the 40-year effort to agree on the *Comprehensive Nuclear-Test-Ban Treaty.* The achievements highlight the prominent contribution that the United Nations, through persistent and long-term effort, can make to global stability and a safer and more secure world. The most prominent recent achievements have been:

- The signature in 1993 and entry into force in 1997 of the *Chemical Weapons Convention (CWC),* which outlawed an entire class of weapons of mass destruction (such as those equipped with the chemical agents: mustard gas, soman, sarin and VX), thus completing a process that started in 1925, when the Geneva Protocol prohibited the use of poison gas weapons.
- In 1995, the States Parties to the 1968 *Treaty on the Non Proliferation of Nuclear Weapons (NPT)* decided to extend indefinitely its provisions. Under the Treaty, States parties undertake to pursue negotiations in good faith on measures to end the nuclear arms race and on nuclear disarmament, as well as on general and complete disarmament. The indefinite extension of the Treaty underscored the broad and growing consensus within the international community on the need for more systematic and progressive efforts toward nuclear disarmament, with the ultimate goal of the total elimination of nuclear weapons.
- In 1996, an overwhelming majority of Members of the General Assembly adopted the *Comprehensive Nuclear-Test-Ban Treaty (CTBT),* which banned underground nuclear-test explosions — an objective originally proposed in 1954 and sought for nearly four decades. The Treaty thus extended the 1963 partial prohibition on nuclear test explosions to all physical environments. With nearly 150 signatory States participating in the Preparatory Commission for the CTBT Organization, located in Vienna,

preparations are under way in the Provisional Technical Secretariat, established in 1997, to ensure that an international monitoring system is operational by the time the Treaty enters into force.

- The signature by over 120 States of the *Convention on the Prohibition of the Use, Stockpiling, Production and Transfer of Antipersonnel Mines and on Their Destruction (Ottawa Convention)* in 1997 is a major step towards addressing the humanitarian crisis sparked by the indiscriminate use of anti-personnel landmines. The Convention marks the first time that a multilateral disarmament agreement bans completely a weapon that is in widespread, active use in the military arsenals of many States. The Convention has spurred the campaign to reduce needless human suffering by increasing resources for mine clearance, mine awareness and mine assistance.

Issue of Nuclear Weapons

In fact, during the cold-war period, a variety of nuclear-disarmament initiatives were put forward, both in and outside the framework of the United Nations, at the unilateral, bilateral, regional and international levels. In January 1946, less than a year after the dawn of the nuclear age, the General Assembly adopted its very first resolution dealing with the issue of nuclear weapons. The International Atomic Energy Agency (IAEA) was established in 1957, to promote the peaceful uses of atomic energy under a system of IAEA safeguards Later, the Agency was given the task of verifying that nuclear material not be diverted for military purposes, as stipulated by the NPT.

Bilateral Agreements

While international efforts to contain nuclear weapons

continued in different forums, it was generally understood that the nuclear-weapon powers held special responsibility for maintaining a stable and secure international security environment. During and after the cold war, the two major powers arrived at agreements that have significantly reduced the threat of nuclear war. In the 1970s, the *Strategic Arms Limitation Talks (SALTI* and *II)* not only performed the vital confidence-building function of keeping the lines of communication open between the two powers, but also resulted in limiting and containing the nuclear arms race. Several bilateral treaties have proved to be important steps towards nuclear disarmament.

Bilateral Agreements

1. The 1972 *Treaty on the Limitation of Anti-Ballistic Missile Systems (ABM Treaty)* limits the number of anti-ballistic missile systems of the United States and the former Soviet Union to one each. A 1997 "demarcation" agreement between the United States and the Russian Federation distinguishes between "strategic", or long-range ABMs, which are still prohibited, and "non-strategic" or shorter-range ABMs, which are not.
2. The 1987 United States-Soviet Union *Intermediate- and Shorter-Range Nuclear Forces Treaty (INF Treaty)* eliminated an entire class of nuclear weapons, which includes all land-based ballistic and cruise missiles with a range of 500 to 5,500 km. By the end of 1996, all the weapons slated for destruction under the provisions of the Treaty had been eliminated.
3. The 1991 United States-Soviet Union *Strategic Arms Limitation and Reduction Treaty (START I)* places a ceiling of 6,000 warheads on 1,600 deployed long-range nuclear missiles for each side by the year 2001, thereby reducing the 1991 stockpile levels by about 30 per cent.
4. The 1992 *Lisbon Protocol to START I* committed the

Russian Federation, Belarus, Kazakhstan and Ukraine, as successor States to the Soviet Union, to abide by the START I Treaty; Belarus, Kazakhstan and Ukraine were to adhere to the NPT as non-nuclear-weapon States. By 1996, these three States had removed all nuclear weapons from their territories.

5. The 1993 *Strategic Arms Limitation and Reduction Treaty II (START II)* commits both parties to reduce the number of warheads on long-range nuclear missiles to 3,500 on each side by the year 2003, and eliminated MIRVed (multiple independently targetable re-entry vehicle) ICBMs (intercontinental ballistic missiles). A 1997 agreement extends the deadline for destruction of the launching systems — missile silos, bombers and submarines — to the end of 2007.
6. In 1997 in Helsinki, agreement was reached to begin START III negotiations on further reductions in nuclear weapons stocks, once START II has entered into force.

Multilateral Agreements

Commonly recognized as the cornerstone of international efforts to contain the proliferation of nuclear weapons, the Treaty on the Non- Proliferation of Nuclear Weapons has near universal membership, including the five States which acknowledged possession of nuclear weapons (China, France, the Russian Federation, the United Kingdom and the United States.) The indefinite extension of the NPT in 1995 made permanent the commitment of the non-nuclear-weapon States parties not to acquire nuclear weapons. It also legally extended the commitment of the nuclear-weapon States parties, under article VI of the Treaty, to pursue nuclear disarmament.

Remarkably, the agreements have been reached to limit the spread of nuclear weapons by prohibiting them from certain environments or geographic regions. For example, treaties have been concluded to prohibit the deployment and testing of nuclear weapons on Antarctica (1959), in outer space (1967) and on the ocean floor (1971).

Concept of Nuclear-Weapon-Free Zones

It must be remembered that in a development that was to herald a new movement in regional arms control, the signing of the 1967 Treaty for the Prohibition of Nuclear Weapons in Latin America and the Caribbean (Treaty of Tlatelolco) established for the first time a nuclear-weapon-free zone (NWFZ) in a populated area of the world. Since that landmark agreement, three other NWFZs have been established: in the South Pacific (Treaty of Rarotonga, 1985), South east Asia (Treaty of Bangkok, 1995) and Africa (Treaty of Pelindaba, 1996). By virtue of such treaties, the whole of the populated southern hemisphere has nuclear-weapon-free status, greatly reducing the chance of nuclear proliferation. Proposals have been made for establishing nuclear-weapon-free zones in Central Asia, Central Europe, the Middle East and South Asia.

It must be remembered that the International Atomic Energy Agency (IAEA) plays a prominent role in international efforts aimed at preventing the proliferation of nuclear weapons. IAEA serves as the world's international inspectorate for the application of nuclear safeguards and verification measures covering civilian nuclear programmes. By the end of 1997, there were some 221 safeguards agreements in force in 137 member States (and in Taiwan, China). To verify their implementation, 200 IAEA experts conduct daily on-site inspections in every part of the world, for a total of some 2,500 safeguards inspections a year. Their aim is to ensure that the nuclear material held in 1,000 nuclear installations in some 70 countries is not diverted away from legitimate peaceful uses to military purposes.

IAEA thus contributes to international security, and reinforces efforts to halt the spread of arms and move towards a world free of nuclear weapons. Various types of safeguards agreements can be concluded with IAEA. Those in connection with the NPT, the Model Protocol Additional to Existing Safeguards Agreements, the Treaty of Tlatelolco, the Treaty of Pelindaba and the Treaty of Rarotonga require non-nuclear-weapon States to submit their entire nuclear-fuel-cycle activities to IAEA safeguards.

Other types of agreement cover safeguards at single facilities. IAEA safeguards under the NPT are an integral part of the international regime for non-proliferation, and play an indispensable role in ensuring implementation of the Treaty.

Areas of Priorities

Though the cold war is over, nuclear disarmament and non-proliferation of nuclear weapons remain the priority concerns in the area of multilateral disarmament. Many Governments, their militaries and the public are weighing the security benefits versus the security risks of the remaining weapons of mass destruction that have not been prohibited by international agreement.

There is a growing body of opinion, in nuclear-weapon and non-nuclear-weapon States alike, that much more rapid progress towards total nuclear disarmament is needed in the years to come. In response to a request by the General Assembly for an advisory opinion on the question of the legality of the use or threat of use of nuclear weapons, the International Court of Justice in 1996 stated unanimously that States are under an obligation "to pursue in good faith and bring to a conclusion negotiations leading to nuclear disarmament in all its aspects".

The adoption of the CTBT in 1996 also added impetus to the momentum in that direction. Many States feel that efforts should focus on the adoption of a time-bound phased programme of nuclear disarmament, while others stress that the States possessing nuclear weapons have made unprecedented progress through negotiations and can continue to do so.

At the multilateral level, efforts will be pursued within the framework of the General Assembly, the Conference on Disarmament and the annual preparatory meetings leading to the next review of the NPT in the year 2000.

On Chemical and Biological Weapons

With the Chemical Weapons Convention, a stringent international verification regime to oversee the implementation of a treaty banning weapons was created for the first time. The Convention established for that purpose the Organisation for the Prohibition of Chemical Weapons (OPCW), located in The Hague, the Netherlands. The OPCW has initiated the international verification regime involving, among other things, the collection of information on chemical facilities on a worldwide basis and a routine global inspection system to verify that States parties are complying with the Treaty's terms.

In the similar vein, the Biological Weapons Convention (BWC), which prohibits the development, production and stockpiling of such weapons, was concluded in 1972 and entered into force in 1975. To build confidence in the effectiveness of the prohibition, States parties exchange detailed information each year on such items as their high-risk biological research facilities.

Since 1995, they have been striving, through the convening of expert groups, to find ways to strengthen the verification of compliance procedures of the Convention. It must be remembere that the geopolitical rivalries of the cold war greatly influenced the entire range of disarmament initiatives.

There was a tendency to highlight weapons of mass destruction to the exclusion of conventional weapons used in conflicts throughout the world, which are no less destructive to human life. The growing proliferation of landmines around the world has been a particular focus of attention. In 1995, a review of the Convention on Certain Conventional Weapons (so-called Inhumane Weapons Convention or CCW) produced an Amended Protocol II strengthening restrictions on certain uses, types (self-destroying and detectable) and transfers of anti-personnel landmines.

Not satisfied with what they considered an inadequate response to a serious humanitarian crisis, a group of like-minded States negotiated an agreement on a total ban on all anti-personnel landmines — the Convention on the Prohibition of the Use, Stockpiling, Production and Transfer of Anti-personnel Landmines — which opened for signature on 3 December 1997 in Ottawa.

Further efforts are being undertaken to make universal adherence to the Convention. It has been proposed that the Conference on Disarmament conduct multilateral negotiations to seek an approach to the total ban acceptable to those States that have not adhered to the Ottawa Convention. The CCW review also achieved a prohibition on the use and development of blinding laser weapons, thus precluding their ever being deployed as weapons of war.

Multilateral Disarmament and Arms Regulation Agreements

- 1959 *Antarctic Treaty,* demilitarizes the continent and bans the testing of any kind of weapon;
- 1963 *Treaty Banning Nuclear Weapon Tests in the Atmosphere, in Outer Space and under Water (Partial Test-Ban Treaty):* restricts nuclear testing to underground sites only;
- 1966 *Treaty on Principles Governing the Activities of States in the Exploration and Use of Outer Space, including the Moon and Other Celestial Bodies (Outer Space Treaty):* mandates that outer space be used for peaceful purposes only and that nuclear weapons not be placed or tested in outer space;
- 1967 *Treaty for the Prohibition of Nuclear Weapons in Latin America and the Caribbean (Treaty of Tlatelolco):* prohibits testing, use, manufacture, storage, or acquisition of nuclear weapons by the countries of the region. All five nuclear-weapon States are parties to it;
- 1968 *Treaty on the Non-Proliferation of Nuclear Weapons (NPT):* the non-nuclear-weapon States agree never to acquire nuclear weapons and, in exchange, are promised access to civilian nuclear power technologies; nuclear-weapon States pledge to seek to carry out negotiations relating to cessation of the nuclear arms race and to nuclear disarmament;
- 1971 *Treaty on the Prohibition of the Emplacement of Nuclear Weapons on the Sea-Bed and the Ocean Floor and in the Subsoil Thereof (Sea-bed Treaty):* bans the emplacement of nuclear weapons, or any weapon of mass destruction, on the seabed or ocean floor;
- 1972 *Convention on Bacteriological (Biological) Weapons (BWC):* places a ban on the development, production, and stockpiling of biological and toxin agents, as well as providing for the destruction of such weapons and their means of delivery. A verification protocol, which could not be elaborated when the Convention was negotiated, is now being considered by the States parties;
- 1980 *Convention on Certain Conventional Weapons (CCW):*

prohibits certain conventional weapons deemed excessively injurious or having indiscriminate effects. The Convention is considered an umbrella agreement, to which additional agreements can be added. As of 1997, it contains four Protocols.

Protocol I bans weapons which explode fragments that are by X-ray undetectable within the human body; *Amended Protocol II* (agreed in 1995) limits the use of certain types of mines, booby-traps, and other devices; *Protocol III* bans incendiary weapons designed to set fire to targets; and *Protocol IV bans* the use of blinding laser weapons;

- 1985 *South Pacific Nuclear Free Zone Treaty (Treaty of Rarotonga):* bans the stationing, acquisition or testing of nuclear explosive devices and the dumping of nuclear waste within the prescribed zone. It has been signed by, among others, all five nuclear-weapon States;
- 1990 *Treaty on Conventional Armed Forces in Europe (CFE Treaty):* limits the numbers of various conventional armaments in a zone stretching from the Atlantic ocean to the Ural mountains;
- 1993 *Chemical Weapons Convention (CWC):* prohibits the development, production, stockpiling and use of chemical weapons worldwide and requires their destruction;
- 1995 *Southeast Asia Nuclear-Weapon-Free Zone Treaty (Treaty of Bangkok):* bans the development or stationing of nuclear weapons on the territories of the States party to the treaty;
- 1996 *African Nuclear-Weapon-Free Zone Treaty (Treaty of Pelindaba):* bans the development or stationing of nuclear weapons on the African continent;
- 1996 *Comprehensive Nuclear-Test-Ban Treaty (CTBT):* places a worldwide ban on nuclear test explosions of any kind and in any environment;
- 1997 *Landmines Convention (Ottawa Convention):* prohibits the use, stockpiling, production and transfer of anti-personnel mines and provides for their destruction.

Peaceful Uses of Outer Space

The United Nations works to ensure that outer space be used for peaceful purposes and that the benefits from space activities be shared by all nations. This concern in the peaceful uses of outer space began soon after the launch of the Sputnik — the first man-made satellite — by the Soviet Union in 1957, and has kept in step with the subsequent advances in space technology.

The United Nations intergovernmental body active as the focal point in this area is the *Committee on the Peaceful Uses of Outer Space,* set up by the General Assembly in 1959 and made up of 61 Member States. It reviews the scope of international cooperation in peaceful uses of outer space, devises programmes and directs United Nations technical cooperation in this field, encourages research and dissemination of information, and contributes to the development of international space law.

The Committee has two Subcommittees:

- The *Scientific and Technical Subcommittee* currently discusses matters such as remote sensing of the earth by satellite, the use of nuclear power sources in outer space, space debris, space transportation systems, space activities related to the earth's environment, astronomy and planetary exploration.
- The *Legal Subcommittee* currently addresses such items as the definition and delimitation of space, ways to ensure the rational and equitable use of the geostationary orbit, and review of the status of the five international legal instruments governing outer space.

The Committee and its two Subcommittees meet annually to consider questions put before them by the General Assembly, reports submitted to them and issues raised by Member States. Working on the basis of consensus, the Committee makes recommendations to the General Assembly.

Legal Instruments

The work of the Committee and its Legal Subcommittee has resulted in the adoption by the General Assembly of five legal instruments, all of which are in force:

(1) The 1966 *Treaty on Principles Governing the Activities of States in the Exploration and Use of Outer Space, including the Moon and Other Celestial Bodies* (commonly known as the *"Outer Space Treaty")* provides that space exploration shall be carried out for the benefit of all countries, irrespective of their degree of development. It seeks to maintain outer space as the province of all humankind, free for exploration and use by all States, solely for peaceful purposes, and net subject to national appropriation;

(2) The 1967 *Agreement on the Rescue of Astronauts, the Return of Astronauts and the Return of Objects Launched into Outer Space* (the *"Rescue Agreement")* provides for aiding the crews of spacecraft in case of accident or emergency landing, and establishes procedures for returning to the launching authority a space object or its components found beyond the territory of that authority;

(3) The 1971 *Convention on International Liability for Damage Caused by Space Objects* (the *"Liability Convention ")* provides that the launching State is liable for damage caused by its space objects on the Earth's surface, to aircraft in flight and to space objects of another State or persons or property oh board such objects;

(4) The 1974 *Convention on Registration of Objects Launched into Outer Space* (the *"Registration Convention")* provides that launching States shall maintain registries of space objects and provide information on objects launched to the United Nations. Under the 1974 Convention, the *Office for Outer Space Affairs* maintains a United Nations Registry on objects launched into outer space. Information has been provided by all launching States and by the European Space Agency (ESA);

(5) The 1979 *Agreement Governing Activities of States on the Moon and Other Celestial Bodies* (the *"Moon Agreement")* elaborates the principles relating to the Moon and other celestial bodies set out in the 1966 Treaty, and sets up the basis to regulate the future exploration and exploitation of natural resources on those bodies.

It is remarkable that on the basis of the work of the Committee and its Legal Subcommittee, the General Assembly has also adopted the following set of principles on the conduct of space activities:

(a) The *Principles governing the use by States of artificial Earth satellites for international direct television broadcasting* (1982) recognize that such use has international political, economic, social and cultural implications. Such activities should respect the sovereign rights of States, including the principle of non-intervention, should promote the dissemination and exchange of information and knowledge, and should foster development.

(b) The *Principles relating to remote sensing of the Earth from outer space* (1986) state that such activities are to be conducted for the benefit of all countries, respecting the sovereignty of all States and peoples over their natural resources, and for the rights and interests of other States. Remote sensing is to be used to preserve the environment and to reduce the impact of natural disasters.

(c) The *Principles on the use of nuclear power sources in outer space* (1992) recognize that such sources are essential for some missions, but that their use should be based on a thorough safety assessment. The Principles also provide guidelines for the safe use of nuclear power sources and for notification of a malfunction of a space object where there is a risk of re-entry of radioactive material to the Earth.

(d) The *Declaration on international cooperation in the exploration and use of outer space for the benefit and in the interest of all States, particularly developing countries* (1996) provides that States are free to determine all aspects of their participation in international cooperation in space activities on an equitable and mutually acceptable basis, and that such cooperation should be conducted in ways that are considered most effective and appropriate by the countries concerned.

The Vienna-based *United Nations Office for Outer Space Affairs* serves as the secretariat for the Committee on the Peaceful Uses of Outer Space, and assists developing countries in using space technology for sustainable development. The Office disseminates space-related information to Member States through its International Space Information System.

Through its United Nations Programme on Space Applications, the Office provides technical advisory services to Member States in conducting pilot projects, and undertakes training and fellowship programmes in such areas as remote sensing, satellite communication, satellite meteorology and basic space science. The Office provides technical assistance to Regional Centres for Space Science and Technology Education affiliated with the United Nations. The Centres help to develop skills and knowledge of scientists and researchers in the aspects of space science and technology that can help to develop human resources for space technology applications and sustainable development.

The Centre in Asia and the Pacific became operational in India in 1995; the Centres in Africa and in Latin America and the Caribbean are expected to be operational in 1998. The Office works in close cooperation with organizations such as ESA, the International Astronautical Federation (IAF) and the Committee on Space Research (COSPAR).

Besides the Office, other United Nations organizations are active in areas such as space communication, satellite meteorology, space science and remote sensing. To coordinate the space activities of the United Nations system, an *Inter-Agency Meeting on Outer Space Activities* convenes once a year.

UNISPACE Conferences

The United Nations has organized two major world conferences on outer space — the *First and Second United Nations Conferences on the Exploration and Peaceful Uses of Outer Space,* held in Vienna in 1968 and 1982. The first conference examined the practical benefits deriving from space research and exploration, and the extent to which non-space countries, especially developing countries, might enjoy them.

The second conference (UNISPACE 82) reflected the growing involvement of all nations in outer space activities; assessed the state of space science and technology; considered the applications of space technology for development; and discussed international space cooperative programmes.

The third conference (UNISPACE III) was convened as a special session of the Committee on Outer Space in Vienna in July 1999. Intergovernmental and non-governmental organizations with space activities as well as space-related industries also participated in UNISPACE III, which sought to promote the use of space technology to solve regional and global problems, and to strengthen the capability of Member States, particularly developing countries, to use space-research application in the service of development and well being of humanity.

GUIDELINES ON CONFLICT, PEACE AND DEVELOPMENT COOPERATION

To improve donors' development efforts, the OECD Development Assistance Committee (DAC) issued a policy statement in May 1997 to provide "Guidelines on Conflict, Peace and Development Cooperation on the threshold of the 21st Century".

The key points include basic principles:

- The basis for sustainable development must be to help a society strengthen its capacity to manage conflict without violence.
- Humanitarian assistance is not a substitute for sustained political commitment in support of peace. This commitment requires the application of all instruments open to the international community - economic, social, legal, environmental and military. Coordinated coherent responses between governments, inter- and non-governmental bodies are also necessary.
- Developing. countries, even in crisis, are responsible for their own development, and the task of international assistance is to strengthen indigenous capacities.

- Development cooperation should seek structural stability embracing social peace, human rights, accountable military forces and broadly shared social and economic development, supported by dynamic and representative political structures.
- Development assistance should seek to address the root causes of conflict.
- Development cooperation should recognize the important role played by women.

The primary objective of development cooperation is to enhance the rule of law and promote popular participation, but specific roles are assigned for different stages of a conflict:

- Before conflict flares, the emphasis is on promoting democratic stability, including attention to arms and military expenditure.
- In open conflict, development agencies should seize opportunities to contribute to. conflict resolution, and plan and prepare for post-conflict reconstruction as well as providing short-term emergency relief.
- In fragile transitional situations, the emphasis should be on saving livelihoods, increasing incentives for peace and promoting reconciliation.
- After conflict, restoring a sense of security is paramount, including restoring legitimate government institutions, encouraging sound macro-economic stabilization plans and taking advantage of opportunities for reform - for instance for participatory debate about the role of the military.

Remarkably, ten key actions for development cooperation include the following:

1. To recognize structural stability as a foundation for sustainable development and advance public understanding of conflict prevention.
2. To strengthen analysis of risks and causes of violent conflict and opportunities for aid to address root causes.
3. To ensure that all policies, including security, political and economic relations, human rights, environment and development cooperation, are fostering structural stability, including support for cease-fires, UN arms embargoes, working to prevent illegal arms supplies and harmonized and responsible behaviour with respect to the supply of military goods, particularly small arms.
4. To strive for greater coherence and transparency by the international community: linking early warning to decision making; coordinating actions; sharing analysis, and agreeing strategic frameworks and responsibility for leadership in coordination.
5. To support regional initiatives for conflict prevention.
6. To reduce budgetary and functional barriers between relief, rehabilitation and development cooperation; reform of the social and economic sectors of the UN system to strengthen synergies in international responses.
7. To work for internationally agreed performance standards and principles to govern operational methods of all implementing agencies.
8. To set up responsive but accountable procedures for resource mobilization, including capacity for crisis management, crisis resolution and ensuring that assistance does not prolong conflict.
9. To promote open and participatory dialogue and

strengthened capacity to meet security needs at reduced levels of military expenditure and strengthened capacity for the exercise of civil authority over military forces.

10. To monitor and evaluate performance in peace and conflict prevention and amplification of best practic.

In the preceding discussion, we have put ample light on the issue of disarmament and its relevance in peace building. If properly implemented with firm determination disarmament policy can play a great role pawing the way for prosperity and development.

In the next chapter we will take the theme—military and strategic security.

9

Military and Strategic Security

A greater poverty than that caused by lack of money is the poverty of unawareness. Men and women go about the world unaware of the beauty, the goodness, the glories in it. Their souls are poor. It is better to have a poor pocketbook than to suffer from a poor soul.

—Thomas Dreier

In this chapter we will address the issue of timely decisions in the field of military and strategic security. The older concepts and tactics of war have changed drastically now. Traditional causes of conflicts have lost meaning. Now wars can be fought on newer contexts.

"All Members [of the United Nations] shall settle their international disputes by peaceful means in such a manner that international peace and security, and justice, are not endangered."

United Nations Charter, Article 2, paragraph 3

From the time that the principle of the peaceful settlement of international disputes was first formulated in the Paris Treaty for the Renunciation of War of 1928 to its latest reaffirmation in the documents of the Meeting of Heads of State or Government of European countries held in Paris in November 1990, more than six decades have passed. However, this period of history cannot possibly be called peaceful. In the World War II alone, more than 50 million people lost their lives besides immeasurable property.

In fact, it would have been expected that after such a shock the efforts of States would have been directed towards the exclusion of war from international relations, towards disarmament. Unfortunately, that did not happen. A new stage of the arms race began, this time nuclear. As a result, humanity—as Mikhail S. Gorbachev put it—very quickly lost its immortality. The nuclear arsenals which have now been accumulated are sufficient to destroy many times over the civilization built up over thousands of years. Yet the process of developing, improving and deploying nuclear weapons all over the planet continues and continues.

No doubt, since 1945 when the United States used nuclear weapons against the Japanese cities of Hiroshima and Nagasaki, nuclear weapons have not been used in war—but hardly anyone would venture to say that they will never be used. Such use could be touched off by some chance event, the unauthorized or provocative firing of a nuclear missile, a technical failure in the means of detection, or a conflict of the kind that recently occurred in the area of the Persian Gulf. More so US's incessant war on terrorism in different regions of the world. It is also disturbing that the number of States which are openly or secretly joining the nuclear club is growing.

The increasing threat of the use of weapons of mass destruction in the course of military conflicts also gives impetus to this process. As such, it must be recognized, without detracting from the importance of declarations on the peaceful resolution of inter-State disputes, that in order actually to exclude war from international relations, something more than declarations is required. What is needed are practical steps. They may be unilateral or taken as a result of international agreements.

However, while the usefulness of unilateral declarations is recognized, it must nevertheless be seen that without negotiations and the specific measures agreed to in them it is impossible to implement the principle of a violence-free world. For Europe, the first tangible steps in this direction were clearly the Treaty between the USSR and the United States on the Elimination of Their Intermediate-Range and Shorter-Range Missiles (INF Treaty) and the signing in Paris in November 1990 of the Treaty on Conventional Armed Forces in Europe (CFE). But, in spite of this major achievement, differences between the approaches of the two sides to the problem of disarmament became apparent in their assessment of these Treaties. For example, in the INF Treaty the USSR agreed, as we know, to eliminate twice as many missiles and almost four times as many warheads as did the United States.

In the Treaty on Conventional Armed Forces it also agreed to eliminate more weapons than any of the other States participating in the negotiations. In doing so, the USSR demonstrated that it firmly supported, not only in words but in deeds, the elimination of the physical basis for the threat hanging over the world and gave practical effect to the new political thinking it had proclaimed, at the root of which, so far as military security is concerned, is the idea of a non-violent, nuclear-free world.

It is apt to mention that the States members of the North Atlantic Treaty Organization (NATO), however, did not see in these Soviet decisions the elements of a new approach to the solution of international problems. Clinging to the stereotypes of the past, they characterized the Soviet Union's agreement to these steps as a "victory", a "triumph", and even the result of the "positions of strength" of the United States and NATO.

This is disquieting—not solely because the assessment

by the NATO countries is groundless. What is alarming is that the apparent emphasis laid on strength in international relations indicates that they have not yet fully grasped the dangers involved in the use of force as a method of solving international problems nor have they taken into account the developing world situation. This conclusion is reinforced by NATO's attitude towards the events unfolding in Europe. It would be logical to expect, for example, that in the wake of the voluntary dissolution of the Warsaw Treaty military organization, the NATO countries would likewise take steps in the same direction—but that has not happened.

On the contrary, there have been declarations about the maintenance and even the extension of the bloc's functions. Nor are the NATO countries in any hurry to revise their military doctrine even to the extent of partial renunciation of the first use of nuclear weapons.

Resultantly, in spite of the first steps taken in the field of disarmament and even in spite of the first unanimous Security Council decision, taken in the case of Iraq's aggression against Kuwait, the construction of a new, non-violent system of international security remains far distant. Just as it is impossible to construct a building on the basis of two different designs, it is impossible to construct a new security system without agreeing on the basic principles of its construction.

The aim of joint decisions should therefore be, not only declarations concerning the rules for mutual State relations, but practical steps leading to the elimination of the physical possibility of "blowing up the world". The first and essential step towards creating the real conditions for a transition to a new system of international security must be a clear statement of the political will of States to renounce the use of force in international affairs.

Further specific steps might then be taken along the lines which can include:

(a) The opposing States and military alliances might agree to renounce attempts to maintain or achieve military superiority over the other side.

(b) They might eliminate their available stocks of weapons of mass destruction. If it is impossible to agree on the complete elimination of nuclear weapons, it might be possible to proceed to their reduction to the lowest level possible. (The opponents of the complete elimination of nuclear weapons consider their retention a guarantee against the possibility that one of the opposing sides might hide or secretly construct a number of nuclear weapons which might be small but would be enough to change the balance of power to its advantage. The retention of a small stock of nuclear weapons, they say, would make such actions pointless. Moreover, nuclear weapons could be used to neutralize the possibility of nuclear blackmail by terrorists.)

(c) The opposing States might decide jointly, by successive agreed reductions in armed forces and armaments, on a basis of military and strategic parity at every stage, to reduce them to minimum agreed levels sufficient only for defence.

(d) While reducing armed forces, the opposing States might give them a non-offensive structure.

(e) The opposing States could work out and put into effect a broad network of confidence-building and verification measures. At the same time, measures would be taken for both the exchange of information and the limitation of the military activities of States.

(f) Inter-State disputes would be resolved by international arbitration, as provided for also in the United Nations Charter and other instruments.

It is significant to note that all the elements of the United Nations machinery responsible for the security of States would be strengthened and, if necessary, new machinery could be created in order to ensure its ability to neutralize any possible attempt by individual States to resort to the use of force in the settlement of inter-State problems. Such machinery could be established under the United Nations and at the regional level—for example, in Europe, side by side with the institutions of the Conference on Security and Co-operation in Europe (CSCE).

In fact, States (and their allies) should be left with only such minimum armed forces as would enable them to retain adequate defensive capabilities while at the same time being unable to carry out large-scale offensive operations. These forces could be structured on the basis of three principles, which would seem in general to meet the needs of the armed forces of opposing States (and their allies) in a non-violent world: military and strategic parity; countering capacity (the renunciation of pre-emptive strikes); and reasonable defensive sufficiency.

In fact, the principle of military and strategic parity is traditionally regarded as the basis for strategic stability and international security. This principle is frequently taken to mean complete equality of military capacity between opposing sides. On that assumption, as has been rightly emphasized by many military and political analysts, the concern for parity becomes one of the factors contributing to arms races to the extent that the opposing sides assess their military capacities differently. As a rule, each of the sides, for various reasons, including inadequate information, somewhat overestimates the potential military capacity of the opposing side and organizes its own defences on the basis of that subjective evaluation.

The other side judges such efforts as intended to gain a military advantage and takes corresponding measures, and so on. In order, therefore, to obviate such subjective perceptions of military parity and their concomitant stimulation of the arms race, it is reasonable to interpret military parity in a somewhat different way.

That is possible to the extent that in present-day circumstances, and particularly given the existence of nuclear weapons, the spectrum of military and strategic parity covers a sufficiently wide range. In actual fact, States adhering to the doctrine of defensive war and renouncing preventive military activities have no need to interpret military parity as strict equality of all military capacities, offensive as well as defensive, of their armed forces with the armed forces of the opposing side (or sides).

It is enough to maintain a balance of military strength enabling a country's armed forces to be confident that they can defend it but not providing them with the physical means to begin large-scale offensive actions for the purpose of aggressive war or to gain political advantage by military pressure on the other side. This interpretation of military parity makes it possible to renounce symmetrical responses to the activities of the other side with respect to armaments, to reduce suspicion that the other side is seeking a military advantage, and to reduce the incentives to over-armament.

Obviously, there is certainly also a need to work out criteria which would make possible an objective assessment of the military strengths of the two sides and enable each side to convince itself that the other did not in fact possess the material means to begin large-scale offensive operations. Measures should also be agreed on to ensure the stability of military parity—which is the most important condition for strategic stability. Such measures would include limiting not only quantitative levels but also the qualitative improvement of weapons and inhibiting the opening of new channels for the arms race.

A necessary first step in this direction is the prohibition of nuclear-weapon tests and the renunciation of the concept of making up for quantitative reductions by the qualitative improvement of the remaining weapons as is done, for example, under the "competitive strategy" of the United States and NATO.

The principle of counteractive capacity implies that States must refrain from preventive military action and pre-emptive strikes of any kind and, of course, from planning for aggressive war. In the words of the Chief of the General Staff of the armed forces of the USSR, Mikhael A. Moiseev, at the Vienna Seminar on Military Doctrines held in January 1990, underlining this principle, a State should "never under any circumstances be the first to take military action against any other State, nor [should] it ever have recourse to such actions unless it is itself the victim of aggression, of an armed attack".

The principle of reasonable defensive sufficiency in the strict sense is hard to discuss without further clarification. Any non-aggressive State can rightly claim that nothing it does with regard to defence is above the level of reasonable sufficiency. Consequently, summarizing the statements made on this score by Soviet officials and filling in the gaps in their statements, the following initial definition might be proposed: "Reasonable defensive sufficiency is a function of whatever problem is under consideration."

Basic Principles

- Reasonable defensive sufficiency, whether with regard to conventional forces or to strategic nuclear weapons, cannot be a fixed quantity or the total of the quantities established for various kinds of armed forces and weapons. Obviously, it must be a function of the ever changing real dangers being faced (including those in existence during the disarmament process) as well as the other factors determining the strategic situation.
- This principle should ensure a defence which, while remaining within the limits of military and strategic parity, would clearly demonstrate to the opposing side the futility of any attempt to settle inter-State questions by force of arms.
- A defence constructed on the basis of reasonable sufficiency should not be excessive. While ensuring adequate deterrence, it should at the same time be limited to the minimum level, including the renunciation of preventive military activities. The defence need not be overloaded with superfluous stocks of weapons and military technology.
- Defence should—and this is very important—be as economical as possible, and should be constructed with due regard for material possibilities and human resources. It should not place too heavy a burden on a country's population.
- The military activity of such a defence, including its military presence on the territory of other States, would be essentially limited. Such a military presence would be permissible only when it was dictated by the need for a joint defence of the States on whose territory the presence was maintained and in accordance with jointly agreed-to obligations. The activity of fleets on world oceans would be reduced. Ultimately, their functions would be limited to maintaining communications and action as part of a United Nations force.
- A defence based on the principle of reasonable sufficiency should not be provocative, that is, it should not lead

neighbouring or other States to strengthen their defensive forces. In order to increase confidence, the transformation of armed forces along these lines should be carried out in conditions of openness and transparency and under the appropriate international supervisory machinery.

- The level of reasonable sufficiency for defence would certainly be dependent on international agreements concerning the limitation and reduction of arms and military activities by the States parties to such-agreements and on the near-term prospects for negotiations.

These measures and principles governing armed forces are, for the moment, no more than proposals which might be utilized in the working out of agreements creating the international legal framework for a non-violent world. They could not, of course, be fully implemented before the questions of security on a regional level, such as European security, for example, are resolved. Nevertheless, a new non-violent European security system is not only possible but necessary. No matter how it is approached, in the final analysis its construction will require the political will of States, the renunciation of military advantage and the maintenance of the three principles referred to above for the constitution of armed forces participating in the military and strategic equilibrium.

Remarkably, as long as the NATO bloc continues to exist, it will of course define the military and strategic situation in Europe. But not only there, for the United States and Canada are also members of that organization, and they can certainly not be called European countries. On the other side, after the voluntary dissolution of the Warsaw Treaty Organization (WTO) as a military organization, the second party to the military balance in Europe in the present circumstances is the Soviet Union.

Accordingly, everything that has been said about the new non-violent system of international security and its establishment on the regional level concerns NATO and the Russia, which for the time being constitute the opposing sides.

The Russia has repeatedly expressed the wish to move from military confrontation towards European co-operation within "a common European home", and it has not only said this but has taken unilateral disarmament and other measures, and has taken bold decisions in the course of negotiations which in fact amounted to further acts of unilateral disarmament.

The heads of the Western States constantly talk about their favourable attitude towards the idea of a peaceful Europe. It is impossible not to believe them, for who now considers war in Europe conceivable? But if that is so, then it is necessary to negotiate on the basis of new approaches, abandoning the centuries-old argument about superior armed forces being the guarantee of security. Unfortunately, the old stereotypes seem to be very much alive. Examples are not far to seek. We need only refer to the negotiations on conventional armed forces in Europe.

The West's intention to secure military advantage for itself through the negotiations was already evident in their proposal for the negotiations. The objective laid down for those negotiations at the Vienna CFE meeting on 9 March 1989—"the establishment of a secure and stable balance of conventional forces at lower levels"—was replaced, at the West's desire, by a balance of land-based armed forces. Conventional naval forces, although they constitute an integral and important part of the military and strategic balance, were excluded from the negotiations. Thus, the as yet unborn agreement was already tipped in NATO's favour.

No special explanation is required for this. To the extent that NATO enjoys significant military superiority at sea, the reduction of land forces to equal levels will transform NATO's military superiority at sea into a general military superiority, which will be all the greater the more radical the land-based reductions are. Consequently, the equalization of the military power of the two sides on land alone will in no way lead to strengthening the security and stability of the balance of conventional forces.

On the contrary, it will lead to the unbalancing of the military potential of the two sides to NATO's advantage—and to the detriment of stability. The argument that naval forces are not the kind of forces that lend themselves to "surprise attack" or in general to use for action in connection with military operations on land does not withstand scrutiny. One need only recall the role played by naval forces in such land conflicts as in Korea (1950-1953), Viet Nam (1964-1973) and the recent events in the Persian Gulf area.

In all these cases the naval forces of the United States played a direct role in the land theatre of operations. It is clear that if NATO continues to ignore the concern of the Russia at the steadily increasing capacity of naval weapons to be employed as well as land forces and land-based aviation for strikes against land targets, including those located far in the rear, further progress in the limitation of armed forces and armaments may be slowed down or even halted entirely. The refusal to negotiate on the reduction of naval armaments must therefore be regarded as an attempt on the part of the United States and NATO either to guarantee their own military superiority or to frustrate the disarmament process.

No third possibility exists. It is noteworthy also that the structure of the Agreement on Conventional Armed

Forces in Europe does not reflect the current situation in Europe: NATO continues to exist and even to expand its functions, while the Warsaw Treaty Organization, as a military and political organization, has ceased to exist. Yet most of the articles of the Agreement were worked out when both alliances existed and the security of the USSR was ensured by the collective forces of all the WTO States. At present, in matters of defence, the Soviet Union can rely only on itself.

Should the Agreement be ratified, as seems likely, the real relationship of forces in Europe, that is, as between NATO and the Russia, will be as follows (to NATO's advantage):

Tanks and armoured combat vehicles 1.5:1
Artillery 1.3-1.5:1
Military aircraft and attack helicopters 1.3:1.

The conclusion is unavoidable: the follow-up negotiations on the strengthening of European security cannot be conducted on a bloc basis. At the same time, the Charter of Paris provides that after the Helsinki meeting scheduled for 1992, negotiations will be conducted among all the 34 States participating in the CSCE process. Those negotiations should become the appropriate forum for the creation of a balance of military power between NATO and the USSR with a view to gradual movement towards a non-violent system of European security.

No matter how perfect the limitation of conventional armed forces and armaments, as long as the two sides continue to possess nuclear weapons, basic security in Europe will be impossible. No equalization of conventional armed forces and armaments can compensate for a surprise nuclear attack. Therefore, while negotiations on conventional armed forces go on, it is necessary to begin parallel negotiations on the elimination or, at the least, the radical reduction of tactical nuclear weapons.

Similar consequences might ensue if the qualitative aspect of weapons is left out of account. If the improvement of conventional weapons and the creation of new categories and types of such weapons is left entirely unregulated, that might radically undermine a formal quantitative balancing of armed forces, with all the ensuing negative consequences.

From that point of view, the qualitative aspect of armaments should also be included in negotiations. It is evident that, as a result of the decrease in international tensions in recent years, the threat of large-scale war, of a nuclear catastrophe, has somehow receded in people's minds, and has become a secondary concern. But wrongly so. The physical basis for war has not been materially reduced.

Military development continues. Further improvements continue to be made in all kinds of weapons, including nuclear weapons. The recent conflict in the Persian Gulf area made it possible to test new kinds and categories of weapons in battle and even gave a new impetus to some programmes which had been slowed down. For example, the successful use of the Patriot anti-missile missile has encouraged the Pentagon to continue work on the Strategic Defense Initiative (SDI). But this means that if a large-scale anti-missile defence system is developed, the first thing to go by the board will be the idea of reductions in strategic and therefore all other types of nuclear weapons.

Whatever its sponsors say about this programme, it can only be assessed by the other side as an effort to obtain a shield ensuring the safety of the United States from retaliation against nuclear missile aggression and by that very token freeing its own hands to impose its will with impunity on any State in the world. It is possible that no such intentions with regard to the SDI programme exist in Washington. But they might arise should the opportunity present itself, and for that reason the other side is obliged to base its own actions, not on words, but on possible practical consequences.

In fact, "efficiency" of cruise missiles has been proved. This once again underlines the need for the strictest limitation or, better still, the prohibition of such dangerous and provocative weapons (which could be armed with nuclear warheads). If before the events in the Persian Gulf some could still dismiss the role of naval armaments in land military operations, no doubt should remain in anyone's mind, after the battle testing of sea-based cruise missiles, carrier aircraft and even naval artillery against land targets, that their role is by no means that of least importance.

The world has witnessed a situation in the Persian Gulf area in which both sides were prepared for the use of weapons of mass destruction, and in consequence the likelihood of a world catastrophe is no longer so remote. All this is evidence that there is no reason for complacency as yet. The problem of the elimination of the threat of war remains as acute as ever and its solution just as urgent.

Though the era of cold war has ceased to exists yet nefarious acts of USA in recent times all over the globe must be condemned by world community. Arms race must be checked and hegemonistic US attitude can be retaliated by gaining economic prosperity by developing world. With collapse of USSR, NATO's role is lessened and India, China, Pakistan, Korea and other countries are as yet forced to strengthen their military power.

The real demand of the hour is gaining economic might instead of military might.

Bibliography

Amos Tversky / Daniel Kahneman, 1981. "The Framing of Decisions and the Psychology of Choice."

Apicella C.L. and all. Testosterone and financial risk preferences. Evolution and Human Behavior. Vol 29. Issue 6. 384-390.abstract.

Bankoff, Greg, George Frerks and Dorothea Hilhorst. 2004. *Mapping Vulnerability*. Sterling: Earthscan.

Birkmann, Joern (editor). 2006. *Measuring Vulnerability to Natural Hazards – Towards Disaster Resilient Societies*. UNU Press.

Bennett, Edward M. *Franklin D. Roosevelt and the Search for Security: American-Soviet Relations, 1933-1939.* Wilmington, DE: Scholarly Resources Press, 1985

Cortada, James W. (2003-12-04) *The Digital Hand: How Computers Changed the Work of American Manufacturing, Transportation, and Retail Industries* USA: Oxford University Press pp. 512.

Cortada, James W. (2005-11-03) *The Digital Hand: Volume II: How Computers Changed the Work of American Financial, Telecommunicati ons, Media, and Entertainment Industries* USA: Oxford University Press.

Cortada, James W. (2007-11-06) *The Digital Hand, Vol 3: How Computers Changed the Work of American Public Sector Industries* USA: Oxford University Press, p. 496.

Damodaran, Aswath (2003). *Investment Philosophies: Successful Investment Philosophies and the Greatest Investors Who Made Them Work*. Wiley. p. 15.

Davis, Robert T. (2010). Robert T. Davis. ed. *U.S. Foreign Policy and National Security: Chronology and Index for the 20th Century*. Praeger Security International Series (Illustrated ed.). ABC-CLIO. p. xiii=xiv.

Diamond, Jared. "Malthus in Africa: Rwanda's Genocide". http://www.ditext.com/diamond/10.html. Retrieved 26 September 2010.

Douglas Hubbard "The Failure of Risk Management: Why It's Broken and How to Fix It, John Wiley & Sons, 2009.

Drake, R.A. (2004). Selective potentiation of proximal processes: Neurobiological mechanisms for spread of activation. Medical Science Monitor, 10, 231-234.

Flyvbjerg, B., 2008, "Curbing Optimism Bias and Strategic Misrepresentation in Planning: Reference Class Forecasting in Practice." European Planning Studies, vol. 16, no. 1, January, pp. 3-21.

Gabriel, Richard, and Paul L. Savage. *Crisis in Command: Mismanagement in the Army*. New York: Hill and Wang, 1978.

Frank Hyneman Knight "Risk, uncertainty and profit" pg. 19, Hart, Schaffner, and Marx Prize Essays, no. 31. Boston and New York: Houghton Mifflin. 1921.

James Franklin, 2001: *The Science of Conjecture: Evidence and Probability Before Pascal*, Baltimore: Johns Hopkins University Press, 274.

Landsburg, Steven (2003-03-03). "Is your life worth $10 million?". *Everyday Economics* (Slate). http://www.slate.com/id/2079475/. Retrieved 2008-03-17.

MacFarlane, S. Neil; Yuen Foong Khong (2006). S. Neil, MacFarlane; Yuen Foong Khong. eds. *Human security and the UN: a critical history*. United Nations intellectual history project (illustrated ed.). Indiana University Press, p. 346.

MAIER, CHARLES S. *Peace and security for the 1990s*.Unpublished paper for the MacArthur Fellowship Program, Social Science Research Council, 12 Jun 1990. As quoted in Romm 1993, p. 5.

McElroy, T., & Seta, J. J. (2004). On the other hand am I rational? Hemisphere activation and the framing effect. *Brain and Cognition,* 55, 572-580.

Obama, Barack. *National Security Strategy, May 2010.* Office of the President of the United States, The White House. Accessed 23 September 2010.

Roberts, Geoffrey. *The Unholy Alliance: Stalin's Pact with Hitler.* Bloomington: Indiana University Press, 1990.

Robin, Ron. *Enclaves of America: The Rhetoric of American Political Architecture Abroad,* 1900-1965. Princeton, NJ: Princeton University Press, 1992.

Romm, Joseph J. (1993). *Defining national security: the nonmilitary aspects*. Pew Project on America's Task in a Changed World (Pew Project Series). Council on Foreign Relations, p. 122.

Rosenberg, David Alan. "Origins of Overkill: Nuclear Weapons and American Strategy, 1945-1960." *International Security* 7, no. 4 (spring 1983).

Rosenberg, Emily G. *Spreading the American Dream: American Economic and Cultural Expansion, 1890-1945.* New York: Hill and Wang, 1982.

Sapienza P., Zingales L. and Maestripieri D. 2009. Gender differences in financial risk aversion and career choices are affected by testosterone. Proceedings of the National Academy of Sciences.

Sayre, Nora. *Running Time: Films of the Cold War.* New York: Dial Press, 1982.

Schaffel, Kenneth. *The Emerging Shield: The Air Force and the Evolution of Continental Air Defense 1945-1960.* Washington, DC: Office of Air Force History, 1991.

Schatz, J., Craft, S., Koby, M., & DeBaun, M. R. (2004). Asymmetries in visual-spatial processing following childhood stroke. Neuropsychology, 18, 340-352.

Schelling, Thomas C. *The Strategy of Conflict.* Cambridge, MA: Harvard University Press, 1960; reprint, 1980.

Schlesinger, Arthur M., Jr. "The Origins of the Cold War." *Foreign Affairs* (Oct. 1967).

Sharnik, John. *Inside the Cold War: An Oral History.* New York: Arbor House, 1987.

Sherfy, Marcella, and W. Ray Luce. *Guidelines for Evaluating and Nominating Properties That Have Achieved Significance Within the Last Fifty Years.* National Register Bulletin 22. Washington, DC: U.S. Department of the Interior, National Park Service, Interagency Resources Division, n.d.

Sherwin, Martin J. *A World Destroyed: The Atomic Bomb and the Grand Alliance.* New York: Alfred A. Knopf, 1975.

Singh, Rickey (13 June 2010). "A USA-CARIBBEAN 'RENEWAL'?" (in English). *Guyana Chronicle.*

Sklar, Robert. *Movie-Made America: A Cultural History of American Movies.* New York: Vintage Books, 1975.

Smoke, Richard. *National Security and the Nuclear Dilemma.* New York: Alfred A. Knopf, 1984.

Snyder, William P., and James Brown, eds. *Defense Policy in the Reagan Administration.* Washington, DC: National Defense University Press, 1988.

Taylor, Gen Maxwell (1974). "The Legitimate Claims of National Security". *Foreign Affairs* (Council on Foreign Relations, Inc.) (Essay of 1974).

Taylor, Maxwell. *The Uncertain Trumpet.* New York: Harper Brothers, 1959.

Thomas, Hugh. *Armed Truce: The Beginnings of the Cold War, 1945-1946.* New York: Athenaeum, 1987.

Thompson, Robert Smith. *The Missiles of October: The Declassified Story of John F Kennedy and the Cuban Missile Crisis.* New York: Simon and Schuster, 1992.

Thywissen, Katharina. 2006. "Components of Risk: A comparative glossary."

Titus, A. Costandina. *Bombs in the Backyard: Atomic Testing and American Politics.* Reno: University of Nevada Press, 1986.

Trachtenberg, Marc. "A 'Wasting Asset': American Strategy and the Shifting Nuclear Balance, 1949-1954." *International Security* 13, no. 3 (winter 1988-89).

U.S. Congress, Office of Technology Assessment. *Technologies for Prehistoric and Historic Preservation.* Washington, DC: U.S. Government Printing Office, Sept. 1986.

Villagran, Juan Carlos. "Vulnerability: A conceptual and methodological review." Source No. 2/2006. Bonn, Germany.

Volberg, G., & Hubner, R. (2004). On the role of response conflicts and stimulus position for hemispheric differences in global/local processing: An ERP study. *Neuropsychologia,* 42, 1805-1813.

Wallace, Mike. "Industrial Museums and the History of Deindustrialization." *The Public Historian* 9, no. 1 (winter 1987).

Walton, Richard J. *Cold War and Counter-Revolution: The Foreign Policy of John E Kennedy*. New York: Viking, 1972.

Weigley, Russell. *The American Way of War*. New York: Macmillan, 1974.

Wells, Samuel F., Jr. "The United States and the Present Danger." *Journal of Strategic Studies* 4, no. I (March 1981).

Wetherell, Charles, et al. "Managing Cultural Resource Information: The California Experience." *Public Historian* 9, no. 1 (winter 1987).

Whitfield, Stephen J. *The Culture of the Cold War*. Baltimore: Johns Hopkins University Press, 1991.

Williams, William Appleman. *American-Russian Relations, 1781-1947*. New York: Holt, Rinehart, 1952.

Worland, Eric John. "Me Other Living-Room War: Evolving Cold War Imagery in Popular TV Programs of the Vietnam Era, 1960-1975." Ph.D. diss., University of California,Los Angeles, 1989.

Yarnarella, Ernest J. *The Missile Defense Controversy: Strategy, Technology, and Politics*, 1955-1972. Lexington: University Press of Kentucky, 1977.

Yergin, Daniel. *Shattered Peace: The Origins of the Cold War and the National Security State*. New York: Penguin Books, 1976.

Young, Marilyn B. *The Vietnam Wars, 1945-1990*. New York: Harper Perennial, 1991.

Zumwalt, Elmo. *On Watch: A Memoir*. New York: Quadrangle, 1983.

Index